BRIAN YARVIN

LANCASTER COUNTY BUCKET LIST

SCHIFFER
PUBLISHING

4880 Lower Valley Road · Atglen, PA 19310

Other Schiffer Books on Related Subjects:

Seasons of Lancaster County, Don Shenk, ISBN 978-0-7643-5755-8
Lancaster County: A Keepsake, Don Shenk, ISBN 978-0-7643-5754-1
Plain Meetinghouses: Lancaster County Old Order Mennonites Gather to Worship, Beth Oberholtzer, ISBN 978-0-7643-5301-7

Designed by Molly Shields
Type set in Poplar Std/ZapfEllipt BT

ISBN: 978-0-7643-5941-5

Printed in China

Published by Schiffer Publishing, Ltd.
4880 Lower Valley Road
Atglen, PA 19310
Phone: (610) 593-1777; Fax: (610) 593-2002
E-mail: Info@schifferbooks.com
Web: www.schifferbooks.com

For our complete selection of fine books on this and related subjects, please visit our website at www.schifferbooks.com. You may also write for a free catalog.

Schiffer Publishing's titles are available at special discounts for bulk purchases for sales promotions or premiums. Special editions, including personalized covers, corporate imprints, and excerpts, can be created in large quantities for special needs. For more information, contact the publisher.

We are always looking for people to write books on new and related subjects. If you have an idea for a book, please contact us at proposals@schifferbooks.com.

To the people of Lancaster County, Pennsylvania. You have welcomed me warmly and taught me important life lessons.

CONTENTS

6 MUSEUMS & HISTORICAL RE-CREATIONS . 106

7 ANTIQUES, AUCTIONS, COLLECTIBLES & UNUSUAL SHOPS............................ 133

THEATER & ENTERTAINMENT 158

SPECTATOR SPORTS 166

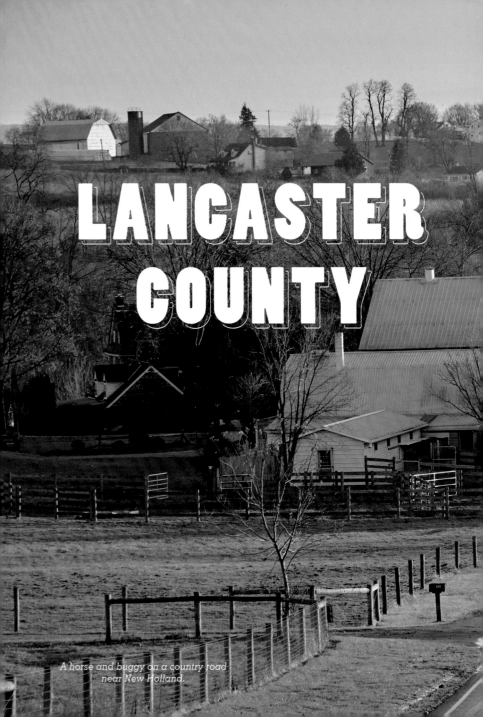

LANCASTER COUNTY

A horse and buggy on a country road
near New Holland.

An Introduction

Lancaster County can be a dream—until you're stuck in traffic behind a string of Amish buggies, eaten yourself sick at a smorgasbord, or the pungent stench of manure creeps into your car during your first visit to a roadside market.

This is a real place with beliefs and passions that run deep. Look, listen, taste, and yes . . . smell.

Some folks have said that all you can do in Lancaster County is stuff your face and pray. You can do that, but there's more. That's why I started writing these things down. Maybe you really did come here for one of those whoopie pies or a few jars of jam. It's just that there's much more to see.

Food is a big deal here. Forty years ago, when most Americans thought there was no better place to shop than the supermarket, Lancaster County promoted itself as a center of local foods and traditional dishes. Then, as the rest of the world became more interested in these things, Lancaster became less so. Some Amish families who had been farming for generations began working in factories or retail stores as their farmland was sold for subdivisions and shopping centers.

Now, though, a whole new group of farmers are reinventing the notion of local food. Produce is organic, meats are pasture raised, and cheeses no longer look like blocks of yellow wax. Lancaster County has regreened.

Our local food resources are exploding with farms, markets, breweries, and restaurants. We also have a thriving entertainment industry, some of the best antiquing in the nation, and outstanding museums.

To people throughout the Northeast, this is Pennsylvania Dutch Country, a.k.a. Amish Country. It's a verdant and pastoral rural area settled by the "Dutch" more than 200 years ago. Not the Dutch from modern-day Amsterdam, but the Dutch in the old English sense of the word. Here's what Wikipedia has to say about it:

> The term "Dutch" is from an archaic sense of the English word "Dutch," which once referred to any people speaking a non-peripheral continental West Germanic language on the European mainland.

Others have said that our word "Dutch" is a corruption of "Deutsch" and that we should really be calling them Pennsylvania German. This book will stick with "Pennsylvania Dutch." It's traditional, commonly used, and almost universally understood.

This is also Amish Country—with residents who are followers of Jakob Ammann, a former Mennonite minister who advocated a stricter cultural separation for his followers in the late seventeenth century. Lancaster was one of the first places in America that the Amish settled, and now their association with the area is deeply rooted in popular culture.

Our Amish community might be only a small percentage of the county population, but their lifestyle and activities are quite visible. Visit them at their farm shops or produce stands and get a firsthand feeling of what it means to live with a deep commitment to faith.

Despite its historic landmarks and remnants of almost every decade of the past two centuries, Lancaster County is not a living museum. Everything and everyone you encounter is modern in some way. The Amish may have chosen not to have cars or televisions, but they have barbecue, tacos, sneakers, espresso, and cell phones.

Wherever you go in Lancaster County, you'll see people who wear distinctive clothing as part of their religious practice: men in black pants and straw hats, women in long skirts, and all sorts of variations. Collectively, they're called Plain people; it's just that their meaning of "plain" isn't the same as ours. Plain people might not wear modern clothing, but they

| Buggy washes at a farm supply shop | Pumpkins at a roadside stand near |
| near Bird-in-Hand | Bowmansville—a typical autumn scene |

never choose their wardrobe randomly. I define them as people who wear specific garments to mark their religious beliefs.

Among the Plain people of Lancaster County, clothing is a powerful signifier. In this day and age of statement fashion, Plain people make the most assertive statement. Their outfits tell their stories: where they are in life and what they believe can be discerned at a glance. Clothes tell us if the person is married or single or belongs to the Amish, Old Order Mennonite, Dunkard, or another Plain sect.

Not all Plain people are Amish. Even locals think the Lancaster Amish are easy to spot, but they are often confused with Old Order Mennonites. If you're looking for the Amish, look for women with solid-color dresses and black smocks, and men with straw hats, black pants, and suspenders.

These outfits have meaning. Jackets without buttons rebel against eighteenth- and nineteenth-century military uniforms. Women's dresses are held together only with pins because snaps or zippers convey a message of modernity they've opposed for generations. Much of it began with modesty in mind, but after a century or two, they stand out in a crowd in a way you might have thought only a sequined blazer could. It may

seem like they're trying to show off by dressing so differently, but that's not the way Plain people see it. Instead, their attire expresses the degree to which they are distancing themselves from modern life.

However, as many Amish move away from farming, this is a difficult struggle. It pits the desire to belong to a faith group against the need to fit into society as a whole. Members see themselves as separate from the secular world, yet they often have jobs that put them in close contact with outsiders.

Transportation is the other big Plain story. Buggies with black sides? In Lancaster County, those are driven by Old Order Mennonites. They're the bicycle riders too. There are Amish settlements in the US where buggies are black, yellow, or white, and bicycles are ridden, but not here. Lancaster County Amish households use buggies with gray sides, and you'll never see them on bicycles. Instead, they get around on kick scooters.

Talk to them if you're feeling up to it. Some, especially those working in the tourist business, will be happy to chat. That doesn't mean they can answer complex philosophical questions—that may require a visit with the experts—but with a bit of effort, those can be found too.

No matter what you do here, you'll find plenty of locals right beside you. We regularly shop at Central Market and the outlets on Route 30. We take our children on tours of local farms and to Dutch Wonderland. Lancaster's fine-dining restaurants might have customers from New York and Washington, DC, but they serve just as many people from the neighborhood. The line that separates visitors from locals is hard to find.

It's time to explore.

Laundry on the line, a common sight in rural Lancaster

Pennsylvania Dutch chicken pot pie

1

DINING

All You Can Eat

Lancaster County's buffet restaurants opened long before our nation began worrying about obesity. During that time, Pennsylvania Dutch Country was trying to sell itself as a land of plenty. Those buffets, called smorgasbords after a legendary style of Swedish food presentation, became an icon of the place. Go to Lancaster and eat! Bring your teens! Join all those hungry, hard-working farm kids and "eat till it ouches." (Yes, this was an expression used to promote one of the big smorgasbords years ago.)

Today, we see these things differently. Too much fast food makes us want to be seated and served. Long battles with weight make us hesitate when we see piles of fried chicken and tubs of rice pudding. And in our daily lives, we are so inundated with food messages that those smorgasbords no longer sing out to us.

So why even note their existence? Smorgasbords level the playing field. That kid who won't eat carrots can just get what he feels like, and as much of it as he wants. The buffets of today are prepared for whoever comes their way and whatever it is they eat. Say no to the fried food, down a quadruple helping of salad, or keep your food fetishes a secret. It's all okay.

What does the word "smorgasbord" even mean? It's the traditional, local name for all-you-can-eat restaurants that feature buffet service.

While the word is an Americanized version of the Swedish word *smörgås-bord* ("sandwich table"), Lancaster County smorgasbords follow no Swedish traditions and almost never have anything Swedish on their buffets.

Apparently, the word goes back to Sweden's pavilion at the 1939 New York World's Fair. There, a restaurant served a buffet called a *smörgåsbord*. It was so popular that the term quickly passed into English. Stripped of its diacritical marks, it became "smorgasbord," an American English synonym for buffet. But in a Pennsylvania Dutch context, it's smorgasbord. Not buffet and no funny little marks over the *o* or *a*.

Two totally different things tend to trip up smorgasbord newcomers. First, don't try to "beat" the buffet. As with any restaurant, it's not the in-dividual dishes you're buying, it's the experience. You don't somehow win by filling up on the most expensive stuff. Instead, you can have a far better time by just eating what you feel like and enjoying the moment. Second, Lancastrians eat early, and even earlier when they hit the buffet. If you wait until 8:30 in the evening, these establishments will be closing.

Is there some sort of hungry past that we want to reconnect with? Are we stuffing ourselves to satiate some sort of primal instinct? Is there some motherly sense of feeling totally and absolutely fed? It's easy to reject ideas like these until you're face to face with all that food.

Shady Maple Farm Market and Smorgasbord

129 TODDY DRIVE, EAST EARL
WWW.SHADY-MAPLE.COM

From a distance, you can see that it's a building on a hill. Sort of an acropolis, or at least a megachurch. It's brick and almost windowless and looks like it could hold a football stadium or two. It's the Shady Maple Farm Market and Smorgasbord.

Shady Maple is a place where too much is not enough. For people who eat in quantity, this is the mountaintop—the land-of-plenty made real. The buffet, the biggest you'll find for a hundred miles around, is on the top floor. Enter the warmly lit lobby. There's plenty of space for people to gather, mingle, and wait for a table. You'll also find a customer service desk; stop here and ask how much your meal will cost and whether discounts and coupons are available. This place isn't cheap, but there's help on offer.

The spread will have you crying for mercy. By the time you reach the center point, where the dishes start reappearing in reverse order, you'll feel like a Shady Maple lost soul, drifting from steam table to steam table. What are your options? Roast beef, baked ham, asparagus, broccoli, mashed potatoes, baked potatoes, corn fritters, baked corn, soups, cakes, pies, and nightly specials such as seafood or barbecue.

There's something for everyone: you can be both picky and a glutton. Gluten-free vegans heap their plates with salads, broccoli, and cranberry relish, while someone at the next table takes nothing but ham. It's like that old country song: "eat like nobody's watching, eat like it won't ever hurt . . ."

After a few bites, you'll notice that everything's good—maybe very good. Yet, nothing is great. You'll start hoping that the next thing you'll try is the holy grail. So you keep eating: big plate of salad with a scoop of that old Pennsylvania Dutch specialty, hot bacon dressing. Then maybe some chicken corn soup. Then the main dishes, and if you've timed it right, the weekend specials. You feel like you can't stop. If you leave something on your plate or just pause for a second, you'll be stalked by the Amish Mafia. Indeed, if the cast of the *Amish Mafia* took you to a restaurant, this is where you'd go.

The place has a Las Vegas feel. For many locals, especially Plain people, it is as close to a casino as they'll get; lines of steam tables instead of slot machines and vats of cooked shrimp instead of roulette wheels. However, you won't find alcohol—and don't even think of bringing your own bottle.

The crowd? Hundreds of people at any given moment. On a Tuesday evening, lots of seniors, young families, construction workers in matching T-shirts, and school groups. All carry massive portions of whatever looked good to them. This is the only place in Lancaster County that I could easily imagine the Rat Pack dining. You almost expect Sammy Davis Jr. and Dean Martin to wander the aisles with big smiles and heaping plates.

Like any Vegas casino, there are people wandering aimlessly, not quite ready to start playing. Not sure where to dig in first? I was one of those people. How about the salad? Follow with fries or corn fritters? Then I looked down and noticed that I had both a New York strip steak and a seared tuna steak on my plate. And then, while sitting at my table a few moments later, I realized that I had somehow eaten them without even making a conscious decision to do so.

Soon, you'll find yourself moving toward the dessert bar, and the crowd will be there with you. No matter what they chose for their meal, everybody will want whipped-cream topping from that hulking steel machine in the back. The men from those work crews and tween girls from local dance teams will pile their plates high with it. I put a bit on my traditional smorgasbord meal ending—a bowl of bright-green pistachio pudding.

If you can still move, there's a gift shop downstairs. Like the rest of the Shady Maple complex, it's huge. Here too you'll find another restaurant, called the Dutchette. You can get a soup and salad bar buffet, a single trip to the salad bar, or a "fill it yourself" taco shell. You can eat your fill here for less than ten bucks a person, something worth noting if you're here buying groceries and run out of steam.

The Shady Maple supermarket is in a building at the bottom of the hill. It has more kinds of potatoes than you ever knew existed, and kinds that aren't even kinds, like "chef potatoes." Even half a year after the harvest, there are still a dozen kinds of apples on the shelves. Summer brings ten-for-$2 cucumbers.

How many kinds of buttermilk? I couldn't count. It's all here: pickled eggs, pigs' feet, pizzelles, tongue souse, whole-grain pasta, and freshly rendered lard. Food is the Shady Maple's theater, and everything is on-stage, from small cylinders of single-serve coffee creamers to huge cans of chocolate pudding.

Push on toward the meat zone, and you'll find pork sausage, beef sausage, turkey sausage, and smoked chicken breasts and legs. Scrapple made from pork or turkey shares a shelf with pan pudding. There's a whole bacon section in yet another aisle, and smoked bones for your dog too.

What in heavens is "Amish blend coffee"? How can there be so many pretzels without any being whole wheat? And those doughnuts. The eating never stops. I leave feeling like a recovering alcoholic who fell off the wagon after a particularly laudable streak of sobriety.

Dienner's Country Restaurant

2855 Lincoln Highway East, Ronks

WWW.DIENNERS.COM

A plate heaped with food at Dienner's Country Restaurant

On a train from New York City to Lancaster, a friend was eavesdropping on a conversation. A lively guy in his nineties was doing most of the talking. After boasting about his amazing life in Pennsylvania Dutch Country, he was asked what his favorite restaurant was. He didn't hesitate. "Dienner's! It's where the local people who love food eat."

This was something I'd heard before. Old-school, rural Lancastarians of a certain age and taste love the place. But for all its popularity, Dienner's presents potential customers with a problem—they close most evenings at 6 p.m. This isn't for a lack of demand. Even when it's bitterly cold or spitting rain, there's a crowd waiting outside. And if that crowd hasn't been seated well before closing time, they'll have to go somewhere else.

The mysteries dissolve once you're inside. It's packed because it's half the price of its more famous competitors, because it has no Las Vegas shine, and because it has ecumenical prayers on the place mats and biblical quotations on the walls. That makes sense when you look at the crowd—more Plain people than most other restaurants, and the rest with local T-shirts from every corner of the county.

I went for dinner on a Tuesday evening. While I was working on a very good piece of ham loaf, I noticed it was 5:45 p.m. Dienner's would close in fifteen minutes, and yet the waiting line was buzzing. Amish ladies were still bringing food out to the steam tables while customers were two or three deep at the main-course area.

Three buffet tables—salad bar, main courses, and sweets—are lined up in the middle of the room. There's also a fridge of pie slices and a soft-serve ice cream machine nearby. It's all you need to serve a Pennsylvania Dutch crowd. Nobody comes here looking for crab legs or prime rib. The "fish and shrimp" on Friday and Saturday evenings is as extravagant as Dienner's gets.

You can also order from a lower-priced menu offering the same foods that you see on the buffet. And of course there are deals—the salad bar with half a chicken at dinner or a quarter of a chicken at lunch gives you the experience without the temptation to overdo it.

When you are seated, a server will put a paper place mat in front of you. Unlike most restaurant place mats of this kind, there are no advertisements for insurance agents or plumbers. Instead, four prayers are offered—Orthodox, Protestant, Jewish, and Catholic. Not being much of a theologian, I silently recited all four.

It was time to eat. It's always a good idea to start with the salad bar. That way, even if you eat absurd amounts of fat and sugar, you got some green in you first. The stars were chopped ham, chopped boiled eggs, and whole boiled eggs cooked in beet juice.

Confident that my body would forgive me for going easy on the salad, I quickly advanced to the main courses. The rotisserie chicken and ham loaf were flavorful, hot, and fresh. Cooked whole red beets were unusual and a perfect foil for the Pennsylvania Dutch sweet treatment. I ate until almost closing time.

I approached the dessert section with only minutes to spare. People were still trying to get in as I went for my raisin pie, and while I picked up my last item—pistachio pudding—a Mennonite lady was locking the doors.

There was no chance to linger. Drinks weren't included in the price, and it was too late to add anything to my check. Out on the patio, I took notes on a small pad and wished I had a cup of after-dinner coffee. Twenty minutes after closing time, people still came to the door hoping to get in.

Since the staff was gone, it fell upon me to tell them the place was closed until morning. I didn't make any friends there.

Dienner's is the real deal. People line up because the prices are reasonable, the dishes are freshly prepared, and the dessert choices are a tiny bit outside the box. Just keep one eye on the clock.

Lititz Family Cupboard

12 WEST NEWPORT ROAD, LITITZ
WWW.LITITZFAMILYCUPBOARD.COM

Many people fondly remember the first time they bought beer without an ID check. It was a benchmark of growing up. The same cannot be said of the first time you were charged the senior-citizen price in a restaurant without having to ask for it. That moment is a bit more depressing. I know the Lititz Family Cupboard as the place where it happened to me. When I asked for my check, the senior price was already entered. I've barely hit retirement age, but I must look as old as I feel. I still go back, though.

Lititz Family Cupboard is a few yards west of a main intersection, and there's plenty of parking. The offerings are solid: a bakery with exemplary pies, cupcakes, and cookies; a menu of modern American favorites with just enough Pennsylvania Dutch mixed in to remind you where you are; and a buffet with a dozen or two choices, all worth a taste. In addition to a basic salad bar, there is rotisserie chicken, meats, more meats, and an array of starches: baked lima beans and baby lima beans, macaroni and cheese, cooked baby carrots, mashed potatoes, and stuffing—called "filling" in Lancaster.

Let a host seat you, and note those prayer place mats. I didn't have the guts to ask my Old Order Mennonite server why there was no Amish or Mennonite prayer. I failed to do this at Dienner's too. I need to gather my courage.

The buffet is a smart choice here. That doesn't mean I wouldn't order off the menu or stop by for a box of cookies. It's just that a good buffet gives you the chance to try something you wouldn't otherwise order. That's what happened on my first visit. It was breakfast time, and we took the buffet with the thought that a big meal at 10 a.m. would hold us until dinner. That was the theory.

After almost filling a plate with the usual suspects, I was stopped dead in my tracks. Right there on the steam table was a dish of pan pudding—a Pennsylvania Dutch specialty I'd seen in butcher shops but had never tasted. Scrapple gets the glory, but pan pudding has even more esoteric roots and, quite frankly, more alien ingredients to fear.

Pan pudding looks like chili con carne but is the color of liver. Without any clue to how it was supposed to be eaten, I spooned some on a piece of toast. It tasted exactly the way it looked, like chili with a tiny bit of liver added. It was a perfect buffet moment. I didn't love it, and it didn't matter. I was happy to have tried it.

Here in Lancaster County, doughnuts are elevated to an art form, and the ones at Family Cupboard make the case. Obviously fried, but without a speck of grease, they are high up in the Lancaster doughnut pantheon. The buffet lets you take as many as you want, which is not something I personally recommend, but something you might want to do once in your life.

The bright-green pistachio pudding I've grown used to seeing on Lancaster County buffets was missing, but in its place was cracker pudding—perhaps the best item I'd yet had in smorgasbord land.

Because it's wedged between Rock Lititz (page 159) and a few Plain communities, Lititz Family Cupboard is one of the few places on the planet where you might see Old Order Mennonites and rock stars dining in the same room. Unflappability is the rule of the day here. Focus on the food and let those contrasts of everyday Lancaster County life wash over you.

Miller's Smorgasbord

2811 Lincoln Highway East, Ronks

WWW.MILLERSSMORGASBORD.COM

I had a plan. Miller's Smorgasbord would be my last buffet visit because it offered two payment tiers: the full buffet, or a less expensive soup-and-salad bar. I'd decided to go for the soup and salad because in the process of creating this book, I'd eaten so much Pennsylvania Dutch food that I was bursting out of my pants. Soup and salad would have been a wise budget move too. Miller's is the most expensive of the Dutch restaurants I visited; it's easy for one person to spend more than $30 here, even for a weekday lunch.

However, I was paraded in front of the entire buffet on the way to my table, and my best intentions went down the drain. While the soups seemed appealing, the salads were minor league compared to the rest of the dishes. I broke down and went for the whole smorgasbord.

Miller's is a tad nicer than the other buffets. It has none of the casino feel of Shady Maple (page 16), and with comfortable chairs, a wine list, and soft lighting, it is far more elegant too. That leaves potential guests in a quandary. For this price, you could eat an excellent meal in one of the better microbreweries that dot the county, and for a few dollars more, Lancaster City's fine-dining restaurants are in the running too.

That said, all the good reasons for eating in a buffet are present here, and in relaxed surroundings. It's fun to eat up a storm in a place like this. Start with two or three soups, then add some pickles and salads. Next, fill a plate with a piece of fried chicken, a turkey croquette, a few meatballs, and a slice of ham with buttered noodles and sautéed kale on the side. After that, a baked apple and a slice of chocolate pecan pie or cheesecake. Yes, you've overeaten, but lunch will last you the rest of the day.

Amish Meals at Home with Samuel and Ruth Lapp

(610) 593-1206, EXT. 0
RESERVATIONS REQUIRED

Visitors to Lancaster County used to experience a special treat—dinner in an Amish or Old Order Mennonite home. You'd head over to a remote farmhouse and find yourself seated at a big table in a small room. There you'd have a huge meal described as Pennsylvania Dutch, with lots of preserved vegetables, a big piece of meat, a couple of starches, and a satisfying dessert.

Afterward, you'd slip the host a few bucks and remember that this was authentic—a big, home-cooked meal. You could describe the thrill of these meals the way visitors to Asia and South America describe street food today—daring, intense, and delicious.

You can't do this now. A few food-poisoning incidents compelled the health department to close down some freelancers, changing the landscape. This left a gaping hole in the marketplace, and Ruth and Samuel Lapp stepped in, opening a home kitchen for the modern era.

There is still some discretion involved. The Lapp farmhouse has no signs. Dinner isn't served every night; Ruth makes the decision on the basis of the number of potential customers. If your party is small, call to ask when space is available. She'll do her best to accommodate you, and believe me, her best is very, very good.

A word of warning: You get what they give you. If you have special dietary needs, you're better off dining elsewhere.

Ruth will greet you as you pull up. That's part farm friendliness and part thoroughness. She has a list and is making sure you're on it. Head in and look around. The dining room has the feeling of a basement dinner party with an Amish twist—long tables with place settings on simple tablecloths, and battery-powered lights overhead.

Both Samuel and Ruth are named as hosts, but the male family members played no part in our dinner. They were around, though, doing chores in the neighboring barn and hitching up buggies. Clearly this was Ruth's territory, with help from her three daughters, all of whom knew their jobs and did them almost silently.

On a summer Monday evening, there were more than twenty guests. Most were in a large group and seemed to know each other. My wife, Maria, and I sat with another couple apart from the main group. This gave us the feeling of being at the kids' table at a particularly boisterous suburban Passover Seder.

There may be a few things on the table when you're seated; we had pickled beets, strawberry jam, butter, and sweet peanut butter spread (see Katie's Kitchen, page 27). Within minutes, Ruth's daughters wheeled up carts with big plates of already dressed salad followed by slices of home-baked bread.

Ruth led us in a moment of silence, and I felt shortchanged. Certainly a meal at an Amish home should open with a serious prayer, but not that night. Soon we were digging into the beets and salad. The couple next to us were a bit bashful about those beets, but with some urging from Maria, they began to pick at them. I looked down and started working on my own plate, and when I looked up again, they had polished off those beets. They were converted.

Main dishes came next. I would call them Middle American for want of a better word. Beef with gravy, boiled potatoes, boiled carrots, and baked chicken with a bit of Russian dressing as a sauce.

The food tasted great, and for all the right reasons: the potatoes and carrots were straight from the garden. The meat was nicely cooked. The Lapp family served food that would have been called "modernist" a few decades ago—perfect ingredients that were prepared without any fanfare whatsoever. This is the simple food that so many people talk about and almost no one ever eats.

It ended with pie, ice cream, and cake. The rhubarb pie was like an ideal Plain person—exemplary and faithful. Along with coffee, there was a pitcher of fresh farm milk. Finally, Ruth and her daughters lined up and sang for us. I had hoped to hear Amish hymns in Old German, but we got modern English instead. This bothered nobody except me. Most of the guests sang along when they could and clearly enjoyed it.

I should have known better. No matter how happy the Lapp women were to entertain guests in their home, their faith and heritage weren't going to be part of the show.

Restaurants & Coffee Shops

Traditional regional cooking has had a tough time. The places that once served it proudly have vanished under the unrelenting competition of the big chains. The following restaurants, however, are enduring examples of above-average American roadside restaurants. A perfect example of a disappearing menu item in this area is stuffed pig stomach. It sounds revolting, but it's really a great big stomach casing stuffed with potatoes and sausage. Even the old-fashioned desserts are declining. Shoofly pie (page 88) is everywhere, yet Montgomery pie, funeral pie, and vinegar pie—once just as popular—are now almost extinct. We all have to pitch in to keep these traditions alive.

I urge you to try one of these restaurants at least once. With warm hearts and sincere effort, the owners do their best to offer satisfying meals based on what remains of the local cuisine. Some, like Town Hall, have a long history. Others are newer but maintain the standard by including at least a few traditional dishes on their menus.

Be aware that pretty much any food you are offered in Lancaster County will be underspiced. Mexican, Indian, and Ethiopian restaurants are particularly noticeable in this regard. The kitchen skills and quality of ingredients are there, but the heat is missing.

C. R. Lapp's Family Restaurant

101 FITE WAY, QUARRYVILLE
WWW.CRLAPPSFAMILYRESTAURANT.COM

Pennsylvania Dutch restaurants seem to offer the same combination of classic roadside food mixed with local sweets and soups; C. R. Lapp's is no exception. What's unique about it, though, isn't something you can eat. While the food here is good and the creamy chicken corn soup is a bit different from what you'll find elsewhere, the best thing about Lapp's is its peace and quiet. No background music, no television, no electronics. It's not specifically Plain, but the mood is plain.

Some people might call this food homestyle, although few homes have deep fryers, and plenty here has been fried. What it is, though, is food made for Pennsylvania farmers—mild, wholesome, and substantial, exactly what you'd want if you'd just spent a day in the fields.

Lapp's can surprise you on occasion. A recent Caesar salad was topped with anchovy fillets. (Not mild at all . . . I know!) Exactly as Mr. Caesar intended. Usually it's easier to find fried grasshoppers than anchovies in Lancaster County, yet there they were.

There aren't many restaurants where you can sit and have a burger and fries in near silence. Virtually the only sounds you'll hear are neighborly conversations. Lapp's isn't advertised as an electronics-free environment, yet the tone is as hushed as a Michelin-starred palace. Not one person had a cell phone out on my first visit. Impulsively, I wanted to see what a Facebook friend was doing on the other side of the planet. Even though nobody said anything, I sheepishly put my phone down a few seconds later. If I needed something to think about, I could find it at the rack of Bible study books by the cash register. Otherwise, I could just calm down, eat my meal, and enjoy the moment.

Katie's Kitchen

200 HARTMANN BRIDGE ROAD, STRASBURG
WWW.KATIESAMISHKITCHEN.COM

Katie's Kitchen bills itself as having "authentic Amish cooking." This is true, it's just that only a few dishes are represented: chicken pot pie, Amish wedding meal, and buttered noodles as main courses, and apple dumplings and shoofly pie among the desserts. Amish grocery stores sell a broad array of spices and flavors, but none of them make their way into the Katie's cooking.

On a recent visit, I ordered the buttered noodles—a plate of rustic, house-made pasta covered with beef stew and stewed tomatoes. The noodles had a handcrafted look, and the beef stew was so tender it resembled the best pulled pork. It was in a mild flour gravy without much seasoning. Then the tomatoes caught my attention. They tasted like chunky applesauce—as sweet as many desserts and totally at odds with any previous idea I had of beef stew. I needed a few moments to understand that those tomatoes were the high notes, the zing of fruit and sugar that makes the dish unique. Katie's Pennsylvania Dutch dishes are so authentic that you need a bit of preparation to figure them out.

Sweet is the taste here. They serve a house-made sugar-added peanut butter spread. In the Pennsylvania Dutch way of looking at food, this wholesome food has been made sweet and therefore improved. Its lingering sugary nuttiness makes you happy and filled with self-loathing all at once.

This wasn't everybody's experience, though. Most of the people at other tables were eating typical diner food—burgers, Caesar salads, and big piles of fries. Katie's lets you make the choice. The Amish girls will be happy with your order no matter what it is. Authentic Amish? Authentic Pennsylvania roadhouse? Authentic diner? They sincerely seem to enjoy every dish on the menu and recite the dessert list as if your order would deprive them of a specific item that they themselves want to eat.

I have never met Katie, but I am assured she exists. Sometimes pies are described as "made by Katie herself." This could mean that the other cooks in the (very crowded) kitchen are not up to her standard. But it doesn't. It's all good, in its own sweet way.

The Speckled Hen

141 East Main Street, Strasburg
WWW.SPECKLEDHENCOFFEE.COM

If you fantasize about interacting with the Amish on their own turf, you'll be pleasantly surprised by their presence at the Speckled Hen—a popular public meeting spot for the Amish in the Strasburg area. With Amish people hanging out like executives on stylish couches, talking business, sipping cappuccino, and perhaps enjoying a green salad, it's the real thing—just not the real thing visitors imagine. If your farm were a twenty-minute walk from the Speckled Hen, you'd do the same.

Coffee here is the sort of light roast that people call "third wave," and the baked goods combine the local aesthetic of sweet with the serious artisanship of the best modern bakeries. Nobody comes to the Speckled Hen for a quick cup of coffee—or a traditional Pennsylvania Dutch meal, for that matter. A pour-over or espresso would better suit the setting, which conveys the sort of rural chic that home-remodeling TV shows try for and rarely achieve.

There is high-end baking here. A brownie or slice of quiche is noticeably better than in many surrounding shops, and the prices reflect this fact. You'll spend a few dollars more for coffee and pie than you would at a diner, but the offerings are well worth it.

Town Hall Restaurant

4315 Division Highway, East Earl
WWW.FACEBOOK.COM

Town Hall Restaurant is so iconic that if someone asked me how Lancaster County was doing, I'd check with Town Hall. It's part of a working municipal building, and the oyster stew and house-made noodles are served just a few feet from the fire trucks. With its 1960s wood paneling and matching chairs, it is evident that nothing has changed since before fast food made its first Lancaster County appearance.

Coffee and sweets at the Speckled Hen. The white square is a homemade marshmallow.

1

It isn't just the decor that makes Town Hall feel like a time capsule; the customers play the part too: big guys in baseball caps, gray-haired women sitting beside them, and everybody in sensible, machine-washable clothes. Take a look at the menu, which they post on their Facebook page every day. For those of us who take regional American cooking seriously, there are some irresistible offerings. Here are Pennsylvania Dutch dishes that you can't find anywhere else, such as rivel soup and a scrapple platter for lunch. And what restaurant serves liver and onions anymore? I ordered it for that reason alone.

The specials board at Town Hall. The same dishes could have been offered fifty years ago.

I also ordered the rivel soup. I knew it only from old local cookbooks. The cup set in front of me contained milk broth with dropped dumplings—a rich, savory treat. I realized I had no way of judging it. Why wasn't it served everywhere?

I keep going back for the traditional dishes. The sausage platter, cucumber salad, and pepper cabbage are good, solid, textbook Pennsylvania Dutch, as are the apple dumplings. The restaurant also lives up to its name as a local gathering place. No topic of conversation is more crucial than the weather, nothing is more important than a high school sports event, and everybody is your friend. What's more, a lot is said without anyone seeming nosy.

On one of my first visits to Town Hall, I was the nosy one. Tables were pushed together in the center of the room, and a birthday party was in full swing. Curious about who would choose to have a birthday at this tiny roadhouse, I looked closer. They were all Shady Maple (page 16) employees. Many of them ordered the smoked sausages, so I did too. It was the right choice.

Mean Cup

398 HARRISBURG AVENUE, SUITE 200, LANCASTER
WWW.MEANCUP.COM

Mean Cup is Lancaster's bare-bones cafe. It has cement floors, distressed wood tables, and faux leather seats. Sit here long enough and you'll see the entire power elite of Lancaster stopping by. Professors, judges, real-estate brokers, a doctor or two. And don't forget the students from nearby

Basic Lancaster city sustenance—
coffee and cake from Mean Cup

Franklin & Marshall College, wearing their team jackets. They don't come here for socializing, though. There are other coffee shops for that.

The place oozes practicality. Sit down in those Naugahyde chairs and get to work. It's so practical that it's hard to imagine any time spent here being wasted. So many people have books open! So many more have deals to be done! Others are reading printouts with numbered lines. What are they? Legal documents? Film scripts?

Everybody has the same goals: a good cup of coffee and the need to be productive. Some get snacks or sandwiches, but they can be a distraction, and the regulars at Mean Cup don't welcome distractions. A trial, an exam, a closing, or maybe even a film shoot awaits. Nobody will bother you here, and sometimes all this intelligence and effort will rub off on you. At those moments, this is the most inspiring place in Lancaster.

Square One Coffee

145 NORTH DUKE STREET, LANCASTER
WWW.SQUAREONECOFFEE.COM

SQUARE ONE CLASSES AND TASTINGS
1132 ELIZABETH AVENUE, LANCASTER

You don't have to feel pressure when you visit Square One, but it's there nonetheless. This is the sort of shop that encourages connoisseurship. Knowing the difference between Guatemalan and Kenyan beans and how they react to different brewing and roasting methods might make you look like a snob or a jerk elsewhere, but at Square One, this sort of knowledge is appreciated.

The people behind the counter know their stuff. Square One has sent competitors to major barista competitions, and at least one has done well. In fact, watching barista competitors on the web will give you a good sense of the attitude this place exudes—that of a welcoming expert ready to guide you to new heights of coffee possibility. If you don't know Monsooned Malabar from Tanzanian Peaberry, you can learn here—and questions are welcomed.

Square One also offers classes at its roasting shop on Elizabeth Avenue. Join one, and the world of coffee will become complex in ways you might never have imagined. The store also hosts "cuppings"—highly structured tastings where the basics of coffee quality are evaluated. This can be a great place to start. They'll give you a sense of how serious you can be about the kaleidoscope of flavors that make up coffee.

I like coming to Square One because it's near Central Market (page 79), and unlike other downtown coffee shops, it's likely to have a seat or two free. That being said, I can sometimes feel ashamed. What if they discover that I really like superdark roast chain-store beans brewed in the sort of stovetop espresso pot that they sell only in Little Italy? What if I'm outed as a guy who throws around the right words but drinks Starbucks when he gets the chance? I'm sure they'll still let me in, but my greeting might be a tiny bit chillier.

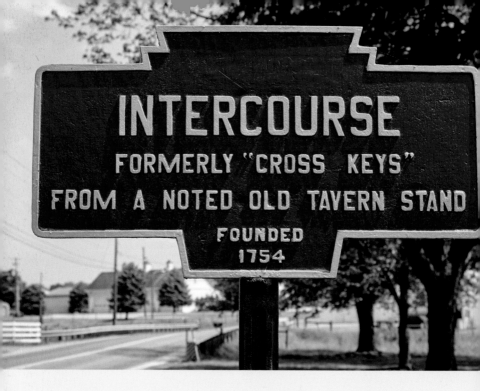

You are now entering the village of Intercourse, Pennsylvania.

2

TOWNS & VILLAGES

Lancaster

WALKING TOUR #1, 1.5 MILES

The neighborhoods that surround downtown Lancaster are worth a walk or two. You can wander through the area, visit a few landmarks, and finish back where you started. Begin at Prince Street Cafe, 15 North Prince Street, across the street from the Fulton Theater.

Heading north on Prince Street, you'll cross Orange Street and pass a parking deck on your right. When you reach West Chestnut Street, you'll see a pocket park on one corner, an old post office building on another, and the Pennsylvania College of Art and Design across the street. Turn left here.

As you reach Mulberry Street, the Shreiner-Concord Cemetery will appear on your left. This is where Thaddeus Stevens is buried, and it's a green, well-tended stop for history buffs. Continue on West Chestnut

Street past St. John's Episcopal Church and turn right on North Concord Street.

The block of Concord between Chestnut and Walnut is a perfect example of Lancaster's many periods, repurposings, and restorations. Start with the modern condos. The details in their front gardens and parking spaces give them a whiff of British influence.

Turn left onto West Walnut Street and make another quick left on North Charlotte Street. This block has long been a place for fine townhomes. Take time to admire the variety of styles.

The 200 block of Prince Street between Orange and Chestnut Streets is known as Gallery Row.

At the end of the block, turn right, heading east on West Chestnut. Pass the Wolf Museum of Music & Art on your right (page 161). Keep walking to the corner of Chestnut and Pine. Here you'll find the Chestnut Hill Cafe, a local specialty coffee shop. Turn left in front of the cafe on North Pine Street.

Continue past Mill, Marion, and Orange Streets to West Grant Street. It's not much more than an alley (as are Mill and Marion), and you'll spot the intersection because it's opposite 551 West, a popular bar and restaurant.

Turn left on West Grant Street, and the mood suddenly changes. In contrast to the leafy residential streets of modern Lancaster, you'll find the mix of housing and industry typical of fifty or more years ago. There's a great example of a warehouse-to-retail conversion at 417 West Grant. Here you'll find the Wacker Brewing Company and the Thistle Finch Distillery offering their products at individual bars in the same large room.

Once you're past the bars, you'll reach the corner of North Charlotte Street. Turn left, walk up the block, and find the punk store—I hesitate to call it a boutique—Angry, Young and Poor (page 138). It's the perfect place to find a gift for the Sid Vicious fan in your life, and a sort of time capsule for a lifestyle that peaked in the eighties and makes surprise reappearances every now and then.

Turn right in front of Angry, Young and Poor and go down West Orange Street. On the block between North Water Street and North Prince Street, you'll find something of a restaurant row. Citronnelle, Sprout, and On Orange are town favorites. On Orange is famous for its brunch menu and almost always requires a long wait. Citronnelle is one of several French fine-dining restaurants downtown, and reservations are essential. Sprout serves Vietnamese sandwiches and noodles in a casual, order-at-the-counter dining space. Feel free to walk in.

After passing the restaurants, turn right on Prince Street, and when you've reached the Fulton Theater (page 162), you've come full circle.

Feel free to improvise your own walks in downtown Lancaster. The grid of streets and back alleys north and west of Central Market makes it easy.

WALKING TOUR #2, ABOUT 0.9 MILES EACH WAY

For some people, downtown Lancaster is nothing more than the Central Market (page 79). But the shopping streets north of Central Market are worth exploring. Things change too quickly to make a directory useful. Instead, we can take a walk down the streets and alleyways that draw the best retailers. Some have their own shops; others set up behind storefronts that resemble the antique malls in Columbia (page 41) and rural parts of the county. Unlike those places, sellers downtown have a sense of style more typical of big cities than malls. With a sharp eye, you'll find something that ticks all the boxes—stylish, fun, beautiful, and reflecting the soul of Lancaster.

We can begin at my usual starting point: Prince Street Cafe at 15 North Prince Street, near the corner of King and Prince. Facing Prince Street, turn right outside the cafe and right again on the narrow alley called Market Street.

At the end of the block you'll find the Trust Performing Arts Center on your left and Central Market on your right. Turn right and walk through the brick pedestrian zone. There you'll find restaurants and shops in a building of residential lofts—formerly Hagar's Department Store. Turn left just before King Street and check out the boutiques on your right. Keep walking until you reach Penn Square. The Lancaster City Visitor

Downtown on Penn Square, Central Market's tower and the Griest building, Lancaster's oldest skyscraper, are distinctive symbols.

North Queen Street looks like a storefront, but it represents a collection of vendors, each with its own display. Building Character offers a similar experience on a grander scale. Turn left through the arches at 342 North Queen, and you'll see the old warehouse building on the right. This place crosses the hip, boutique atmosphere of Madcap (and the rest of the neighborhood, really) with the structure of an antiques mall. Our tour ends at the corner of North Queen and East Lemon Streets.

Georgetown

ROUTE 896 SOUTH OF STRASBURG

HOMETOWN KITCHEN

18 FURNACE ROAD, QUARRYVILLE

WWW.EATATHOMETOWN.COM

STOLTZFUS ANTIQUE FURNITURE

7 LANCASTER AVENUE, QUARRYVILLE

FISHER'S HOUSEWARES AND FABRICS

1098 GEORGETOWN ROAD, PARADISE

HOMESTEAD GROCERIES

1046 GEORGETOWN ROAD, PARADISE

Is there a holy grail for Lancaster explorers? Something that everybody searches for and nobody finds? For me, it's a real Amish town. A place where residents and businesses are dominated by the Amish without the trappings of tourism. It's a dream that's tough to realize. While there's some disagreement, it seems that the Amish make up about 10 percent of Lancaster's population, not enough to make a separate village.

With its concentration of Amish businesses, Georgetown comes close. Its location, south of Strasburg on Route 896, is a bit confusing. Driving toward Georgetown from the north, you'll see a sign that says "Village of Georgetown" and a small post office marked "Bart, Pennsylvania" a few yards away.

Both names describe the same place. The annual mud sale (page 154) is in Bart, while the popular Hometown Kitchen places itself in Georgetown. Either way, it's exactly the same place. To further confuse visitors, the postal and GPS addresses of businesses in town aren't Bart or Georgetown; they're Quarryville or Paradise. Hometown Kitchen and Fisher's Housewares are only a few yards apart and have different town names in their addresses.

This isn't a perfect small town—it has a subdivision and a drive-through bank—but it does the trick. There's an Amish department store, a cafe, a market, and a sprawling used-furniture business, plus a small tavern and a post office. And even though it's not Lancaster's Brigadoon, it's a great place to stop, stroll, and have a meal.

Start at Hometown Kitchen. This is a modern Amish restaurant—the Amish take on small-town American food. Eggs for breakfast, burgers, salads, sandwiches, and a handful of platters for dinner. Don't expect much in the way of old Dutch cooking except for apple dumplings, shoofly pie (page 88), and maybe a bowl of chicken corn soup. It's not adventure eating, but it's perfect for locals who want something filling during a busy workday.

Stoltzfus Antique Furniture occupies parts of three buildings at the Georgetown crossroads. Avoid the collectibles, small gifts, and fancy ornate pieces and look for the good, solid-wood furniture, often in need of a tiny bit of loving care. There are so many tables, shelves, and different kinds of cabinets that I often wish I had an *Antiques Roadshow* appraiser along to tell me how they were used. As with so many Lancaster County antique stores, you have to keep going; giving up before you've explored every last nook and cranny will be your loss.

With only gas lanterns for lighting and aisles so narrow you have to slide through sideways, Fisher's Housewares and Fabrics might seem like a convenience store for the Amish. Instead, it's a superstore filled with items they use—oilcloth, plastic tableware, and huge pots, for example. It also carries uniquely Amish items such as religious books, sacred texts written in Old German, and Amish romance novels. This is the place to buy Amish clothing too. Whether it's a hat or coat or bonnet you're coveting, come here for the real thing.

Homestead Groceries is the neighborhood's Amish convenience store. Here you can find bulk foods, canned goods, and repackaged kitchen items from Costco. Like Fisher's and the furniture store, you won't find electric lighting. Browse the dimly lit aisles for spices, inexpensive vitamin supplements, and other things used to keep an isolated rural household of ten or twenty people fed and well.

And that's it for Georgetown. The countryside encroaches without any buffer. It may not be an Amish town, but it's a town the way the Amish like it. Farms, a few houses and shops, and before you know it—farms again.

Columbia

WEST OF LANCASTER ON ROUTE 30
REGULAR BUS SERVICE FROM DOWNTOWN LANCASTER
EXCEPT ON SUNDAYS

When people tell you that Lancaster city is too hipster, too snooty, and just plain too expensive, they're almost always comparing it to Columbia. It's the poor man's Lancaster city, the sort of town where tattoo parlors outnumber coffee shops. Settled by Quakers, it lacks any trace of Plain culture. If you zip through, you won't see much going on, but poke around and you'll notice that many old industrial buildings have become antiques malls where vendors offer every possible sort of collectible, and interesting furniture too.

Most people start there. If you don't know the drill, they're large spaces with booths for individual dealers. You take whatever catches your eye to a single register, and the cashier and dealers work things out afterward. Columbia isn't the only place in Lancaster County with this setup. There are even more antique shops in Adamstown (page 135), but this is the one town where you can stroll between them.

You don't even have to go inside. The last time I visited, I found a tourist buggy and an old pickup truck for sale in a parking lot. Inside, you'll find what might best be described as the leftovers from earlier times. Giant wooden teeth sit next to hand-painted metal giraffe heads. Old industrial clothing hangs in one spot, while ladies' wool coats are on display a few steps away.

You'll need a very good eye to spot things that are rare and valuable. That being said, one man's junk is another man's treasure. Somebody might desperately want an old, large-format photo enlarger, a boxed set of brass scale weights, or a rotary phone.

If you visit Columbia in good weather, it's worth heading down to the river. The Columbia Crossings River Trail Center offers restrooms and trail information for people who want to walk or bicycle upriver from town. Starting north of the center, a rail trail heads north through Marietta along the Susquehanna River.

That same River Trail Center offers a great view of the Columbia-Wrightsville Bridge (properly called Veterans Memorial Bridge). This long, graceful span is a masterpiece of 1920s engineering. Some say it's the world's longest concrete, multiple-arch bridge. It is beautiful in summer twilight, but bridge and civil-engineering fans will love it in any weather.

Another building of interest is the Market House. Built in 1869 and looking like a gigantic brick quonset hut, it has housed indoor food and farmers markets. Long ago, it buzzed with energy but today is on its last legs.

Wright's Ferry Mansion is a short walk from downtown. Fans of historic houses will want to see its nicely restored interior. The Buddhist

A typical Columbia antiques mall building. Don't hesitate to go on in.

A loft repurposed as an antiques mall in Columbia

temple across the street is worth a look too, although it's open sporadically. A must-stop for museum fans is the National Watch & Clock Museum, which is interesting enough to warrant its own entry (page 107).

In 2014, *Smithsonian* named Columbia one of the twenty best small towns to visit in America. Columbia may be a bit down on its heels, but for antiques fans and river trail enthusiasts, it's heaven. You just come here and do what you came to do. No frills whatsoever.

Intercourse

INTERSECTION OF ROUTES 340 AND 772

KITCHEN KETTLE VILLAGE
3529 OLD PHILADELPHIA PIKE
WWW.KITCHENKETTLE.COM

STOLTZFUS MEATS
14 CENTER STREET
WWW.STOLTZFUSMEATS.COM

OLD ROAD FURNITURE
3457 OLD PHILADELPHIA PIKE
WWW.OLDROADFURNITURE.NET

Intercourse might not be the only town in Lancaster County with a cute name aimed squarely at the tourist trade. But let's face it, this is where Plain and tourist cultures collide. Intercourse is a gentle introduction for people who came to Lancaster for a Bible story show and outlet shopping and think they might want find out about those folks who are always dressed in black. More than that, it's a great starting point for people with mobility impairments. People who could never dream of making it through Old Windmill Farm (page 50) can at least get a sense of things here.

Before the age of tourism, the town was called Cross Keys because two thoroughfares cross here. Real-estate developers renamed it Intercourse in 1814. There are places to park, walk around, shop, see and meet Plain people, and even spend the night. And because it's surrounded by Amish settlements, you'll see horses and buggies trotting down the streets on daily errands.

Much of the town is given over to a combination outdoor shopping mall and bed-and-breakfast inn called Kitchen Kettle Village. There are shops and food stands at Kitchen Kettle, and the north and northeast views from the parking lot are perfect Amish Country scenes.

A short distance away, Stoltzfus Meats on Center Street is an excellent and well-organized butcher shop, and a host of galleries and gift shops make for a pleasant shopping stroll.

Fans of barnwood furniture will appreciate Intercourse. You can wander between shops along Route 340, including E. Braun Farm Tables (page 146) and Old Road Furniture. Their tables, chairs, shelving, and other items attract a large and loyal following. You can also find shop after shop such as the Treasure Place at Smucker Village, across the street from Kitchen Kettle, filled with the sort of rustic modern items you see on TV remodeling shows.

Intercourse is pretty much the only town where quilt buyers can browse and compare price and quality between shops, although the diligent can pay less at mud sales (page 154), and the lucky can sometimes find deals at farm-based quilt-and-craft shops (page 141).

If you spend too much time here, you might get the feeling that not all is quite right: the subliminal message of tacky optimism; the notion that your life can be made better with a birdhouse, a quilt, or some farm-inspired decor can overcome the best of us here. When this happens, take a deep breath and remind yourself that this isn't anything more than a shopping center. You'll be all right.

Intercourse is a great last stop before leaving Lancaster. You can pick up all the things you missed while you were out exploring. Maybe a beautiful skein of yarn at the Lancaster Yarn Shop. Maybe some jams or pickles. Or something more esoteric perhaps. A saddle? Whatever catches your eye, a last stop in Intercourse can also get you one more pretzel and a trip to the restroom before a long drive home.

Vendors at Kitchen Kettle Village in Intercourse

There is one more thing that makes Intercourse uniquely Lancastrian—those shops close early. It might be nice to stroll Kitchen Kettle Village on a cool summer evening, but it's just not in the cards.

Lititz

INTERSECTION OF ROUTES 501 AND 772

Twenty minutes north of Lancaster city, Lititz—population 9,000—is a village with small shops, a park, cafes, and museums. It has none of the grit of downtown Lancaster (page 35), nor does it have suburbia's chain stores and malls.

Named after a castle in the current Czech Republic, the town would be called Litice if spellings had been standardized in the 1700s. In those days, Pennsylvania was filling with all sorts of religious groups from northern Europe, and not just Amish. The Moravians who settled Lititz were looking for a place to worship, practice a deep pacifism, and create a community.

One thing you'll hear about Lititz is that it's "cool," a reference to the rock-and-pop-music culture centered in Rock Lititz (page 159), the charming park in the middle of town, and the strip of high-quality, one-off shops and restaurants on East Main Street between Broad Street and the Moravian Church.

Locally owned stores along Main and Broad Streets contribute to Lititz's small-town charm.

While the entire town of Lititz belonged to the Moravians at one time, today the church holdings are far smaller. The church sits on its own elegant square along East Main Street. Start your visit at Church Square, with its shady, green lawn surrounded by history. In addition to the church, there's the Linden Hall School—once a Moravian girls school and now one of the nation's best all-girl prep schools. Across the street are two museums, one devoted to pretzels and the other to Lititz history. The Moravians own a gift shop on the east side of the square.

As you walk down Main Street, the storefronts start to look fancier, but on closer inspection, they reflect the modesty of the area's first farmers. One store invited me to "indulge!" with "fun socks." I saw groups of Plain Mennonites and groups of prep school girls, each in their respective uniforms. Reserve rules the day: boutiques and thrift shops can be hard to tell apart. Lititz may be built on rock and roll, but it doesn't look like those rockers shop here. Even the most expensive stuff has an air of practicality.

The main shopping district makes a sharp right at Broad Street. North of the intersection of Main and Broad is Lititz Springs Park, a large, grassy space famous for its holiday festivals and decorations. Holiday visitors might wonder how a town park can put up religious decorations. It's because Lititz Springs Park is owned by a nonprofit supervised by the Moravian Church and managed by a board largely run by local churches with zero government input.

Next to the park, the old Wilbur Chocolate Factory also helped put Lititz on the map. The company's distinctive, flower-shaped Wilbur Buds, introduced in 1894, were made there until 2016, when the operation moved elsewhere. The factory has since been repurposed for mixed use, including luxury condos and a hotel. But you can visit the Wilbur Chocolate Museum and retail shop across the street, near another Lititz landmark— the Julius Sturgis Pretzel Bakery.

An afternoon in Lititz is time well spent. Its stores are fairly junk free, its food and drink is tasty and fun, and the streets and park are great for strolling. Keep an eye on the calendar too. There are festivals and weekly farmers markets of the sort you'd associate with much-bigger cities.

Come stocked with change for the parking meters! No credit cards are accepted, and spaces off the main streets are used by the locals. It's a popular place.

Buggy on Broad, Lititz

Food and games at the Denver Town Fair.

3

ATTRACTIONS, FARMS & FESTIVALS

Old Windmill Farm

262 PARADISE LANE, RONKS
WWW.OLDWINDMILLFARM.COM

When you turn down the lane that leads to Old Windmill Farm, you'll see miniature horses, a stand with locally made foods, and a shop with Amish refrigerator magnets and the like. It's a bare-bones Pennsylvania Dutch tourist spot, but it isn't yet Old Windmill Farm. For that, you'll have to go another few hundred yards down the driveway.

The welcome sign on the white barn tells the story. Park behind it and ring the big bell by the goat pen. Jesse or Anna, who run the farm, will come and start a tour for you soon enough. While you wait, listen to what other people say as they get out of their cars. "This is exactly like what my grandfather's farm was like!" and "There are real baby animals here!" are typical. Children leap out of back seats, running toward the sheep and turkeys. It's a working farm and not a petting zoo, and even toddlers know the difference.

Old Windmill Farm is completely without pretense. It is not prettied up for outsiders. Simply taking care of the crops and feeding the animals keep this large family busy.

Tours often start in the barn. Those Amish horses look harmless when they're pulling a buggy, but they are a tiny bit intimidating up close and indoors. And one look at the mules and you'll never wonder where the phrase "stubborn as a mule" came from. No animal's face says "I'm not listening to you" the way a mule's does.

If you've read a few Amish romances or seen *Witness* one too many times, Old Windmill Farm will snap you back to reality. Jesse enjoys watching participants milk the cows. Even if it's only a squirt, getting visitors to have some hands-on animal experience matters. With only four cows, all of this dairy is for the family table, but not always as milk. Tour participants sometimes get the chance to make butter too.

Turkeys and chickens are free ranging in the best sense, and sheep and goats live there too. It's not all animals. A vegetable garden in back is large enough to provide for this big family for many months out of the year.

The idea of a season for everything isn't just poetic here; it's the day-to-day reality. Maybe piglets were just born, or maybe a turkey is going to be slaughtered. The smells and sights might be a bit much if you're the

Amish dresses hanging out to dry at Old Windmill Farm

sort who thinks that eggs come out of the chicken as clean as they appear in the supermarket. Think of Old Windmill Farm as a next step in your locavore education. You won't forget the sights, sounds, and smells.

Dutch Wonderland

2249 LINCOLN HIGHWAY EAST, LANCASTER
WWW.DUTCHWONDERLAND.COM

Dutch Wonderland, the amusement park on Route 30, oozes childish exuberance. Rides in sixties-bright colors, a garden with animatronic dinosaurs, and a monorail give the place a feeling that's sometimes cartoonish and always a little innocent. Indeed, at first glance it looks like it hasn't been remodeled since the first season of *The Jetsons* aired. Cynics can think of it as being stuck in the past, but preservationists see something else entirely—a 1963-style amusement park in a near-perfect state. Even when they update the place, the design aesthetic remains sixties television cartoon. Fans of Googie and Popluxe design will find a visit to Dutch Wonderland worthwhile even without setting foot on a ride.

The castle came first, back in the early 1960s, when Earl Clark, a local businessman, had the idea for an amusement park. It's a perfect example of what somebody would have thought kids liked when John Kennedy was president. Then the monorail—that favorite mid-twentieth-century vision for public transportation—came, and the stage was set. Clean and well maintained, at quiet moments Dutch Wonderland seems like a museum.

Clark was a major booster of Lancaster County tourism. Not only did he build Dutch Wonderland, he also created a neighboring campground, a long-gone movie theater and wax museum, and the Amish Farm and House (page 61).

The bright colors and noise can captivate—or perhaps overcaptivate— the most introverted child. Luckily, Dutch Wonderland has something for every mood. Cranky? Princess Brooke will read them a story at one of the theaters. Buzzing? Have them dig for fossils in the biggest sandbox you've ever seen. Overheated? Take them to the child-sized water park.

Adults, particularly those with a historical bent, can study the craft that goes into keeping this place the historical treasure it is. When your kids are on the space-themed rides, note how they reflect the optimism of the sixties. And check out the railroad covered bridge and giant pretzel, the two most obvious reminders of the day when the park was filled with those Pennsylvania Dutch references.

Many people think of Dutch Wonderland as a tourist trap. They see the castle and monorail from Route 30 and can't imagine otherwise. Not exactly. A high percentage of visitors are local. The crowd includes Plain families whose children embrace Princess Brooke and Sir Brandon with the same enthusiasm as everybody else. That local crowd has bred some serious tradition. There are third-generation employees and third-generation season pass holders. It's a treasured local landmark.

Things move at child speed. The cable car that crawls over the grounds gives you plenty of time to check things out. The shady grove of animatronic dinosaurs entertains, teaches vocabulary, and gets everybody out of the hot sunshine. Management has done the thinking, and you and your family can have a vacation that won't upset anybody.

I must warn you, though. The castle gift shop has the biggest collection of princess costumes in this part of the solar system. Just so you know.

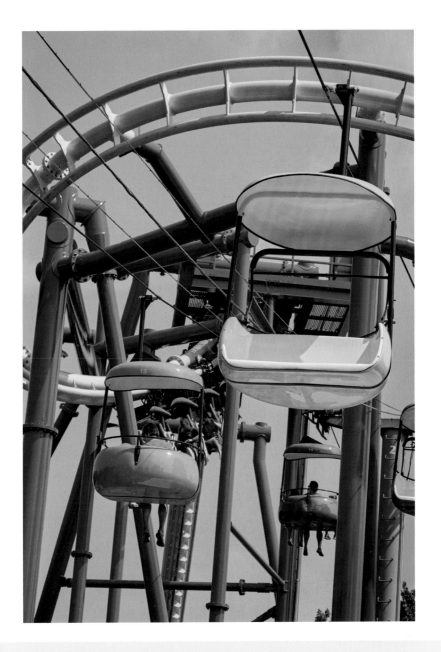

The bright colors and geometric lines of Dutch Wonderland

Verdant View Farm

429 Strasburg Road, Paradise

www.verdantview.com

Some people have specific ideas about what a farm visit should be like. The farm should be as clean as a children's book illustration, the guides should be the farmers themselves, and they should be able to answer any questions you have, no matter how technical, theological, detailed, or obscure. And there's more! People expect meal service, overnight stays, birthday parties, weddings. Forget it! No working farm is odorless, and unless they double as a professor, most farmers don't have that sort of knowledge to share. Something has to give.

A friendly goat at Verdant View Farm

The best compromise I've found is Verdant View Farm. It has tours, a bed-and-breakfast inn, basic workshops, and a rudimentary store that sells the farm's dry-aged beef. Fields of crops surround the barns, along with cows, goats, and chickens. Tours are often given by college students with majors other than agriculture, but they can offer solid and clear answers to many questions about farm life basics.

Paradoxically, the farmers offering visitors the most authentic experience are often the least able to answer questions. So many people do things in a specific way simply because that's the way they were taught. The last person who remembers the reasoning behind a method or tradition may have passed away long ago. Sometimes, we have to step away and do our own research.

You can get close to the animals. The first thing you'll learn is that they're tame, but not pets. A cow isn't a big cat, and a goat isn't a dog with horns, but each is approachable in its own way. Observe how they live and the role they play. Every animal has a job to do.

More than any other farm that's open to the public, Verdant View is just plain pleasant. Stroll the grounds, listen to sounds of livestock going about their business, and take a good look at the fields in every direction. Rounding out the idyll, steam trains from the Strasburg Railroad (page 116) come chugging through once an hour or so. On a hot day, buy a bottle of water from the shop fridge.

There's a balance at Verdant View that one can appreciate. If you're the sort who thinks big thoughts, Verdant View Farm is a solid metaphor for Lancaster County. It's rooted in farming, welcomes tourists, and has a bit of shopping.

That's who we are, right?

Town Fairs

LATE SUMMER AND EARLY FALL BETWEEN LABOR DAY AND COLUMBUS DAY. DATES, TIMES, AND LOCATIONS VARY.

Local fairs are about more than fried food and kiddie rides. Farmers and gardeners take them seriously. Prizes are awarded for horses, cows, pigs, chickens, sheep, goats, and even rabbits, all of which are groomed to the teeth.

In the early afternoon, before the crowds started gathering, the Denver Fair was nothing but a muddy field of mostly closed rides and vendors. There was a Lions Club food stand and a T-shirt guy working in almost dead quiet. The only sound was a bingo game in a distant tent.

Inside one tent were plates of freshly picked, raw vegetables—all too perfect to be believed. String beans, cherry tomatoes, even Napa cabbage. And the Indian corn! Even the best farm stands can't match the corn that's been entered in competition—rows of red, yellow, brown, and black kernels in patterns that don't seem natural at all.

Denver Town Fair

American fairground food, with its obsessive deep-frying, has developed a bizarre reputation. People who don't go to fairs love to hate it. And folks who go love it enough to keep the vendors coming back. I love enough of it to look forward to partaking, and hate it enough to limit my intake. It's a balancing act. I counsel other visitors to take the same approach and sample one or two items.

Then it's time to settle in for some livestock judging. At the Denver Fair, the sheep were so perfectly groomed and sheared that I couldn't tell them apart. I studied their faces and gleaned nothing. Some seemed to know they were being watched.

During the moments before the judging, the crowd grew, but the goats still outnumbered the fans. I studied the goats, listened to the judge, and applauded. It wasn't exactly riveting, but it was better than most movies.

The judge not only knew livestock but had a whole vocabulary of jargon to back it up. His use of the word "expression" threw me. At first I thought he meant the look on their faces, but he was referring to the way a particular animal reflected the ideal of the breed. In this context, faces didn't have expressions, but loins did.

I started to see my favorite cuts of meat in the creatures I studied—legs and roasts and chops. I was overwhelmed by conflicting desires to become a vegetarian and open a butcher shop. In one enlightened moment, I understood why people choose one or the other.

As with everything else in life, the best moments at the fair aren't what you'd expect. Forget the midway games and food stands, and talk to the farmers about what makes a certain tomato or apple special.

I was in a quandary. If I'd had an empty freezer at home, I could have bought a goat and had it slaughtered, butchered, and packed. It would have been great, but I'm sure my wife and I would have grown tired of eating the five or six goat dishes I know how to cook, long before the meat began to show signs of freezer burn.

Don't ignore the music. What you'll hear at fairground stages is the music local people love. Heavy metal and Christian pop covers might show up, but authentic bluegrass can take center stage too. Country music in all forms is popular in Lancaster County, and the best local talent will be on hand.

The biggest challenge facing fairgoers is finding the fairs. Some events have web pages or are mentioned on local first-responder sites. Between Labor Day and Columbus Day, check the event listings of the local newspaper. Otherwise, watch for signs and investigate if you see a cluster of rides and livestock trailers. That will be it.

Buggy Rides

I'll say it officially. Those tourist buggies are the best way to get a sense of the countryside around the small towns of Paradise, Bird-in-Hand, and Intercourse. You move slowly and see a lot. Walkers and bicyclists get a good view, but buggy rides give you a chance to concentrate. You won't worry about your aching knee. You won't have to think about where you're going, and you can have a pleasant chat with the driver.

There are many people who think a buggy ride is too touristy or corny. I once felt that way, and I know better now. Those touring buggies aren't exactly the same as the buggies used by Amish and Old Order Mennonites, but they're the same height and speed—enough to give you a good sense of what it's like to travel that way.

My first piece of advice for potential riders: sit near the driver. Most are Plain people with a lifelong Amish Country relationship. Don't be afraid to ask questions, and don't be surprised when they can't answer. My questions started with the crops we were passing. I learned that the local soil is great for growing soybeans, but it takes a sophisticated machine to harvest them. That's why a field of soybeans is the easiest way to identify a non-Amish farm, according to our buggy driver. A modern operation can rent the gear required to cultivate them efficiently and make them profitable.

Even without a guide, you'll recognize many different kinds of crops. Everybody knows corn, and a close look at the large family vegetable gardens along the route revealed cabbages, broccoli, and asparagus. Pumpkin patches appear later in the season.

You'll see other horse-drawn transport, including Amish families, loaded work wagons, and plenty more tourists too. Only grouches resent the tourist buggies. Indeed, if you attend big Amish events such as Farm Days (page 122) you'll see Amish parents using the big buggies as kiddie rides. Everyone seems to love them.

How do you choose between the many buggy rides on offer around Intercourse, Bird-in-Hand, and Strasburg? By avoiding package deals that include destinations. The reason to take a buggy ride is to take a buggy ride. A simple 2- or 3-mile journey is just right for most of us. A few operators offer longer rides, but remember that 3 miles in a buggy isn't much quicker than 3 miles on foot. If you want to visit an authentic Amish farm, Old Windmill Farm (page 50) will give you a tour. If you want cookies, head over to the Central Market (page 79), where several vendors will exceed all expectations. Keep it simple and always check local visitor magazines for coupons!

There is no rush or thrill on a buggy ride—just the clomping of the horse and the bumping and shaking of the buggy. Absolved of the need to navigate the complex web of back roads between Routes 340 and 23, the trip was a new perspective on a neighborhood I'd passed through many times. I even discovered a hardware store I never knew existed. And everyone waves! The locals seemed to appreciate our interest.

The first thing we did after disembarking and getting back into our car was to retrace the route. We had to look carefully to recognize sights we'd seen just twenty minutes earlier. The road was the same, the buildings were the same, and the Amish kids who waved at us were still at their farm stand, but somehow, everything looked different. We were no longer part of the landscape.

Kreider Farms

1461 LANCASTER ROAD (ROUTE 72), MANHEIM
WWW.KREIDERFARMS.COM

Lancaster County's family farms are small and endearing, with baby animals for children to pet and perhaps evenings of goat yoga for their parents. At the other end of the spectrum are the huge factory operations that provide most Americans with their food. Then there's Kreider Farms, Lancaster's most in-depth agricultural tour. If you want to know how milk gets from a cow to your local supermarket, this is your place. Our guide insisted that there were 3,000 cows and seven million chickens on the farmstead. I didn't count but saw no reason to disagree.

The tour (reserve in advance) starts with a short video at the visitor center, then moves to a bus. You don't wander freely at Kreider Farms;

you're driven from place to place with a guide who has a massive and meticulously prepared collection of moo and cow jokes. It's more appealing than it sounds. After a few sharp turns on rural roads, you enter one of the biggest barns you're likely ever to see. There they are, hundreds of cows—all pregnant—whom the guide adoringly described as the "girls."

As the bus crawled through the barns, the guide reeled off rapid-fire facts and bovine humor. I loved it, and being in

One of several barns at Kreider Farms, housing hundreds of cows

the bus meant I was spared the sight of tourists trying to pet the cows as if they were big dogs. We finally stopped at the milking barn, where a mob of cows filed into a chute that led to a merry-go-round-style milking machine. Like passengers on a big-city rapid-transit system, they seemed focused and organized as they calmly boarded the machine. The moo jokes stopped as we watched hundreds of gallons of milk flow into the tanks. Farm hands, real-life Mr. Greenjeans types, were keying information into computer terminals as the cows took their ride.

It took me a few minutes to notice—or not notice—the lack of stench. Those 3,000 cows produce 150 tons of manure a day, and if it weren't handled carefully, it would be a disaster. The manure passes through a Bion waste disposal system and a huge pond called the Moo Lagoon.

This combination of recycling and self-sufficiency looked to me like a modern manifestation of the "waste not, want not" values of traditional American farming. It was comforting. I wanted to hate this empire of farming, but I had to admit that they were pouring an enormous amount of money and effort into doing things well.

Absent from the tour, but in buildings that were clearly visible, were those seven million chickens. Disease spreads far more quickly among the chicken houses than in the cow barns on the other side of the farm, we were told. For that reason, the birds are off-limits.

Fortified with free samples of chocolate milk, we were taken back to the visitor center. I was struck by the difference between this tour and all the others—Kreider's is part of America's food supply. Its milk and eggs are sold in mainstream stores. Nothing special at all. Yet, this chance to see food production in action is pretty special after all.

Amish Farm and House

2395 COVERED BRIDGE DRIVE, LANCASTER
WWW.AMISHFARMANDHOUSE.COM

The Amish Farm and House is wedged between a Target and a storefront where you can pay your cable bill, and you'd be forgiven for assuming that this is the worst visitor destination in Lancaster County. You'd be perfectly within your rights to ask why a tourist farm on the edge of a strip mall should even exist.

It turns out that the house and exhibits have been in this spot for more than sixty years, one of the first tourist destinations in the county. Early on, it was surrounded by fields, and then parking lots for the visiting crowds. Then a developer bought the land to build a shopping center and was somehow convinced not to demolish the farm. With that, the perfect, tourism/shopping destination was born.

At first I was too cynical to see it. But wouldn't people who come by charter bus want to visit a pleasant farm re-creation and a big-box store in one go? I dare you to visit the Amish Farm and House without at least wondering if you need something from Target.

Here you'll find the clearest, most comprehensible introduction to Amish life that exists. Ask the guides anything. They know what's coming. They're locals with insider insights, but also students of the Amish faith. There are many places you can ask about Amish clothing, but this is the only one where an expert will pick up a garment on a hanger and point out the details, one by one.

Locals come for the legendary goat yoga. What better place is there for this popular fitness activity than a farm, although personally I don't understand the appeal of a goat climbing all over me while I'm working out.

Amish Village

199 HARTMAN BRIDGE ROAD, RONKS
WWW.AMISHVILLAGE.COM

I didn't mean to get into an argument at the Amish Village. However, I had come to expect serious information from the guides at every tourist spot I visited and was disappointed when the one here hesitated. I backed off quickly. It's not that people who know the difference between the Amish and Mennonites aren't welcome, it's that the place isn't prepared for those sorts of questions.

The Amish Village is more amusement park than museum. It is so much fun that a group of four adults immediately pretended to be teachers

This barnside mural marks the entrance to the Amish Village.

and students in the one-room school. Nobody was pondering the philosophy of Amish education. Outside, even the free-range ducks and turkeys seemed to be in a good mood. It's a play village, after all.

I had a good time at both the Amish Farm and House and the Amish Village, it's just that both don't add up to enough. Why is there no real Amish or Mennonite museum in Lancaster County? While the Lancaster Mennonite Historical Society contains interesting archives, it doesn't offer the depth that seems to be called for. Why isn't there a place with scholarship and a proper historical collection? If we can make the commitment to a State Railroad Museum (page 111) and to the re-created village at Landis Valley (page 129), we can give the Amish, Mennonites, and Brethren whose values underpin this entire region a special museum too. The knowledge is there and the demand is great.

Lancaster Farm Sanctuary

558 MILTON GROVE ROAD SOUTH, ELIZABETHTOWN
WWW.LANCASTERFARMSANCTUARY.ORG

Animals of all sorts work in Lancaster County, and sometimes that work doesn't go well. When it turns into overwork or even abuse, there should be a safe place for those animals to go. Despite the many successful sanctuaries around the US, Lancaster hasn't had one until recently. Then, in 2017 two local women, Jonina Turzi and Sarah Salluzzo, inspired by what they'd seen in New York's Hudson River valley, bought a former hobby farm near Elizabethtown.

The women told me that they try to focus on the most typically farmed animals and cases of extreme abuse or neglect. You can see on their faces that they are invested in the emotional lives of these creatures.

Because of that, Lancaster Farm Sanctuary is both a happy place and a sad place. Happy, because there is healing going on, not only for the animals, but for the people who care for them. Sad, because we know the animals have experienced pain.

You may hear repeatedly that farm animals aren't pets, but the sanctuary is a magical exception to the rule. It's not the lap of luxury, but a cocoon of kindness and a place to heal.

For Turzi and Salluzzo, this is a labor of love. Both of them make their living running separate businesses, but the ranks of volunteers and donors for Lancaster Farm Sanctuary are growing, as is the number of events and programs they offer. The sanctuary is open to the public only during special events; check the website.

Rising Locust Farm

1339 Creek Road, Manheim
www.risinglocustfarm.com

Rising Locust Farm is a refreshing reminder that not all Lancaster County farmers use the same crop cultivation methods their great-grandparents did. This operation is devoted to permaculture—a philosophy of agriculture based on using the land's natural characteristics and ecosystems.

On an open farm day recently, I was ready for serious discussion. Before I could ask how a farm could represent the natural history of Pennsylvania when none of its major crops were native to the area, I was interrupted by a small boy who demanded that his mother buy him one of the farm's rabbits as a pet. The boy stood on my left and his mom on my right, and I was caught in the middle.

Eager to escape the family drama, I followed a group of visitors to the hog wallow. Rising Locust Farm pigs seem to be smiling buddhas—not just humanely treated but behavioral role models for their human farmer friends. There were almost twenty nursing piglets split between two moms.

Herds of sheep and cows were in the distance, and I pondered their happiness. It was too good, too pure. I desperately wanted a big bottle of diet soda and a half-dozen chocolate doughnuts. As one of the farmhands talked about how wonderful those sheep were, I tried to calculate how far I was from the nearest can of Spam. Those of us who saw the movie *Babe* know that pigs exist simply to produce bacon, but Rising Locust Farm is so idealistic that you are forced to reset your thoughts. My questions were about sausages and chops, but I was also wondering if I'd reached nirvana.

Toward the end of my visit, I sat and talked with resident farmer Jono Droege about permaculture and the future of farming. The very

A piglet in the hog wallow at Rising Locust Farm

embodiment of the modern homesteader, he seemed out of place among his Plain neighbors and suburban customers. As he sat there in shorts and a T-shirt, flying insects circled him but didn't bite. He clearly had a special bond with living things. Was he the buddha?

I tried the native-crops question again. Droege pointed out that anything cultivated isn't truly a native species because human selection plays a role. That made sense. I remembered that I once bought both wild and farmed pawpaws at market and compared them. Cultivated won.

If you're the sort of person who cares about meat quality and wants to buy directly from the best farms, you can visit the farm shop by appointment (call ahead for a farm tour too). Serious cooks will find leaf lard, jowls, and liver in the freezer. The rest of us can get steaks to put on the grill or chops to toss in a hot cast-iron pan. Vegetarians can buy the farm's unique, forest-grown shiitake mushrooms. If you can't get to the farm, there's a pickup spot in downtown Lancaster. Call to ask, and they'll bring what they can.

After I left, I was driving as fast as I could toward the nearest whoopie pie shop when I felt something crawling up my pants. A creature from Rising Locust Farm had hitched a ride. I started slapping my left leg and noticed big brown splotches on my pants where those bugs were hiding. I headed straight home to shower and change. Rising Locust Farm had left its mark. There were no whoopie pies that day.

Groundhog Day at the Slumbering Groundhog Lodge

SLUMBERING GROUNDHOG LODGE
248 WHITE ROCK ROAD, KIRKWOOD
HOME.PTD.NET/~MSVITALE/INDEX.HTML

On the morning of February 2 at seven o'clock sharp, my car's dashboard thermometer read 2 degrees above zero: pretty cold for Lancaster County. It was Groundhog Day, and at the crack of dawn I was heading to the festivities at Slumbering Groundhog Lodge. I'd seen the place before, a large building with a bigger parking lot set on a hill above White Rock Forge Covered Bridge (page 70). What I'd never seen there were the people.

Groundhog Day is a favorite Pennsylvania Dutch winter tradition, and we take those traditions seriously. The beliefs behind it are simple: if a designated resident groundhog sees its shadow, there will be six more weeks of winter. If it doesn't, spring will come early.

Celebrating Groundhog Day on a bitterly cold February morning

Led by a man known as the Hibernating Governor, Slumbering Groundhog Lodge claims that its resident prognosticating groundhog, Octoraro Orphie, has a perfect record of weather forecasting going back to 1908. I was in no position to debate this.

Despite the bitter cold, the place was buzzing. There were men of all ages drinking twelve-packs of canned beer with great enthusiasm, lines seven deep at the many porta-potties, and men walking around with bottles of whiskey and plastic cups filled with ice.

If you're not a county kid, or if you're not from the Mid-Atlantic region of the US, you might not know that a groundhog is a rodent the size of a small dog that lives in underground burrows. Locals also call them woodchucks. There are other names, but the list is too long to enumerate.

Orphie may have a perfect record of prognosticating, but he appears to be stuffed. Also stuffed is Mount Joy Minnie. She's the mascot of an annual Groundhog Day parade 30 or so miles northwest of the lodge. Lancaster's other Groundhog Day festival was at a downtown bar that claimed no resident rodent at all.

Mount Joy Minnie wasn't my type, so there I was, in the remotest parking lot in the county, watching as a handful of men took the podium. All were wearing the white coats typically seen on food-industry workers. This gave the impression that I was watching a lineup of butchers. One stepped onto a small wooden floor laid out on the snow, and another began to play the banjo. Flatfoot dancing! And good dancing too!

As is often the case, I was a pioneer, the only male with a container of coffee instead of the hard stuff. However, many of the women had thermoses filled with hot drinks, some so large that I couldn't imagine how they brewed enough coffee to fill them. Everyone carried a container of some sort.

While we were drinking, the parade started. Fifty or sixty men, all in those white butcher's coats, black top hats, and assorted groundhog paraphernalia, began marching through the covered bridge. I expected the audience to cheer and clap, but they just stood there and sipped.

Soon, other white-coats began reciting poetry—experts might describe it as cowboy poetry about groundhogs in general and Octoraro Orphie in particular. The noise, crowds, and biting cold were rolling into one painful experience when the speakers began proclaiming Orphie's prediction of more winter. Between you and me, any creature short of a polar bear would have noticed that winter wasn't going anywhere, but the folks in the white coats loved their little, stuffed groundhog and weren't going to give a shred of credit to anyone else.

All this was a parody of some sort. The Slumbering Groundhogs reminded me of the water buffaloes on the *Flintstones*. With a bit of research, I found out that they were poking fun at the private lodges American men once flocked to. They populated the American landscape in the days before television and video games. Lancaster apparently still has Masonic, Elks, and Moose lodges, so somebody must remember.

The members of Slumbering Groundhog had indoor refuge and plenty to drink, but not the rest of us. I recorded Orphie's prediction on my little notepad and headed back to my car. Some people looked like they were on the edge of freezing to death, but the only complaint I heard was the lack of Octoraro Orphie paraphernalia for sale. I wasn't the only one who'd have sprung for a scarf.

Covered Bridges

Bridges made of wood planks, heavy beams, and a roof over the roadway are known as covered bridges. These distinctive designs were created to protect the load-bearing structure and make maintenance easier. A hundred and fifty years ago, they were the height of practicality; today they're a quaint relic.

People love the bridges. Some are attracted by the huge bent-wood beams, testament to the kind of engineering that lives on only in these painstakingly restored structures. Others assume, and rightly so, that the bridges are in areas of great natural beauty. Because Lancaster is a patchwork of sprawl, industry, and magnificent agrarian scenery, seeking out covered bridges will often get you to the most-bucolic spots.

Lime Valley Covered Bridge

Most of the covered bridges named here are on county or town property and are being used for their original purpose. Some no longer perform that job but have been preserved as parts of tourist attractions.

Covered bridges are disputed, argued about, rebuilt, renamed, and even moved from place to place. I've used the names given to them by Google Maps. The names might not be historically accurate, but it's a widely known mapping system that we can all find on our phones and laptops.

Sadly, you can't visit all of them. Some are on narrow roads where cars can't pull over, and parking on front lawns or stopping in the middle of the road creates a hazard for other travelers, so don't do it.

Some people consider covered bridges so romantic that they call them "kissing bridges." This means that wedding parties, photo shoots, and other life events can easily fill those parking spots. I always enjoy seeing this kind of activity, even if it means a detour.

Two of Lancaster County's covered bridges stand out as parklike destinations in their own right. Poole Forge Covered Bridge sits on property owned by a private nonprofit. It's in superb condition, easy to find, and a perfect spot for a picnic or even a wedding. Kurtz's Mill Covered Bridge is in Lancaster County Central Park (page 96) and has a lawn and parking area.

Landis Covered Bridge is a popular spot not far from downtown Lancaster. Quietly tucked behind a strip mall, you'll find fishermen working the stream and kids from the nearby condos playing in the grass. Although this is a modern setting, the scene was probably the same a century ago.

Willow Hill Covered Bridge is a modern structure made from pieces of two condemned bridges. It's by far the most conspicuous, sitting on private property between the American Music Theater and a Panera Bread shop on Route 30. Paths lead to it from either parking lot. It's not the most scenic spot, but it's there—one more way Lancaster repurposes its history.

Oberholtzer's Mill Covered Bridge is on private land in a campground. Check with the office before you spend more than a few minutes there.

Each bridge is listed on the chart with a nearby street address and star rating. The rating is based on the quality of experience you can have, and isn't a judgment of the structure itself.

One star: the bridge is in a location where it's difficult or impossible to stop.

Two stars: The bridge is surrounded by private property, but there is a roadside pullover for a car or two. Feel free to stop and take a close look.

Three stars: The bridge is in a park or has plenty of parking and is at least partially surrounded by accessible land. Choose these for picnics and rest breaks.

Note: The street addresses listed are for GPS navigation; they are not the bridge address.

Lancaster County Covered Bridges

Bridge Name and Closest Address	Rating	Comments
Amish Bridge (Pinetown Bushong's Mill Covered Bridge) 499 Bridge Road, Leola	**	
Baumgardener's Covered Bridge 88 Covered Bridge Road, Pequea	**	
Bitzer's Mill Covered Bridge 198 Cider Mill Road, Ephrata	*	
Bucher's Mill Covered Bridge 106 Cocalico Creek Road, Stevens	*	
Buck Hill Farm Covered Bridge Private Property	*	Not open to the public
Colemanville Covered Bridge 41 Fox Hollow Road, Pequea	**	Parking on Fox Hollow Road, not at the bridge
Erb's Mill Covered Bridge 78 Erbs Bridge Road, Lititz	**	
Eshelman's Mill Covered Bridge 345 N Belmont Road, Gordonvill	**	
Forry's Covered Bridge 817 Bridge Valley Road, Columbia	**	
Hunsecker's Mill Covered Bridge 1335 Hunsicker Road, Lancaster	**	
Jackson's Sawmill Covered Bridge 1093 Mt Pleasant Road, Quarryville	**	
Kaufman's Distillery Covered Bridge 793 W Sun Hill Road, Manheim	**	
Keller's Mill Covered Bridge 103 Middle Creek Road, Lititz	**	

Kurt's Mill Covered Bridge 21 Kiwanis Drive, Lancaster	★★★	In Lancaster Central Park (page 98)
Landis Covered Bridge Shreiner Station Road off Plaza Boulevard, Lancaster	★★★	Easy access and next to shopping center; look for kitchen appliance store on left
Lime Valley Covered Bridge 300 Brenneman Road, Willow Street	★	
Mercer's Mill Covered Bridge 3771 Bailey Crossroads Road, Atglen	★★	
Neff's Mill Covered Bridge 2099 Penn Grant Road, Lancaster	★	
Oberholtzer's Mill or Red Run Covered Bridge 877 Martin Church Road, New Holland	★	In a private campground; ask in office before an extended visit
Pine Grove Covered Bridge 1 Ashville Road, Nottingham	★★	In an industrial setting with power generator on one side
Poole Forge Covered Bridge 131 S Pool Forge Road, Narvon	★★★	In a historical park
Schenk's Mill Covered Bridge 696 S Erisman Road, Manheim	★	
Shearer's Covered Bridge 504 E Adele Avenue, Manheim	★★★	In a public park next to a school
Siegrist's Mill Covered Bridge 4193 Siegrist Road, Mount Joy	★	
Weaver's Mill Covered Bridge 1680 Weaverland Road, East Earl	★	
White Rock Forge Covered Bridge 248 White Rock Road, Kirkwood	★★★	Site of the local Groundhog Day festivities (page 66)
Willow Hill Covered Bridge 2417 Lincoln Highway East, Lancaster	★★	Between a shopping mall and a theater (page 69)
Zook's Mill Covered Bridge 1049 Log Cabin Road, Leola	★★	

*A roadside table offered spectacular tomatoes to those
who could stop quickly enough.*

4

FOOD SHOPPING

Roadside Stands

At the end of April, the countryside is still mostly brown and gray. A few brave families might stock the makeshift sheds at the end of their lane with pastries and canned goods. Come May, though, the farm stands begin to open.

First up are stalks of rhubarb, and then asparagus. As the season progresses, the shelves fill. Zucchini, cucumbers, and delicacies of all sorts: those buttery greens the Pennsylvania Dutch call "cut lettuce," and zucchini flowers, which local farmers don't eat but for which chefs and passionate amateurs will pay top dollar.

You can find roadside fruit and vegetable vendors all over the region, but Route 625 is prime produce territory. It starts a few yards east of Shady Maple in East Earl (page 16) and meanders north through Bowmansville. That stretch has a reputation as a cook's paradise. Many farms have eggs, and they are strangely inconsistent: some are smaller than you've ever seen, and some are big enough to be called "jumbo" if they made an

Freshly picked corn at
a roadside stand

A bushel of apples at a roadside stand—a great
bargain for shoppers who can use them all

appearance in the supermarket. Live with these variations and you will be rewarded with extraordinary flavor.

By the beginning of August, roadside stands overflow with everything from blueberry pies to garlic. There are days when you'll want to stop at all of them, spending every last bit of cash in your wallet. On a recent trip down Route 625, hanging signs offered melons, peppers, sweet corn, plums, peaches, and cherries. At Ja-Lin Produce, the melons were stacked high, almost hiding the corn. At Red Barn, a horse-drawn cart was delivering cantaloupes. Wayside Produce displayed its bounty in a shed surrounded by startlingly chartreuse tobacco fields.

This is also peak tomato season. Beefsteaks are the name of the game. The multihued heirlooms you see in fancy city markets might be grown here, but they're not always sold on roadsides. Instead, the classics are abundant in red and yellow, ready for eating in just about any form. As delectable as they are, at moments like this I imagine the farmers selling their best produce at such places as Lincoln Center, and all my old New York City friends checking out piles of juicy Cherokee Purple or Black Cherry varieties.

We're here in Lancaster, though, and even off Route 625 there are plenty of finds. Get past a farm town such as New Holland or Bird-in-Hand and take a random turn. There might be a clue—a sign pointing to a quilt shop or household auction. It could be your field of dreams if your dream is fresh vegetables.

By the middle of September, the summer vegetables are pretty much gone and broccoli matures. Look for long, slender stalks. The short, fat crowns you see in the supermarket won't hold a candle to these. Pumpkins start showing up before the official start of fall, but by October they're everywhere. There will be apples and maybe even a few pears, but you'll have to pass the pumpkins to get to them. Every farmer wants to put on a show, and the only script they have is pumpkins—bright orange gets those fine folks from Philadelphia and New York to take out their wallets.

Keep making those random turns until you find what you're looking for. It may just be a crate by the side of the road. You'll pass it by and have to find a place to turn around and go back. If you're truly cursed, in the time it takes to turn around, somebody else will have found the heads of cauliflower you identified as your own. Life is a journey, and often that journey leads down farm lanes.

I stopped at a stand that seemed surrounded by a vast moat of pumpkins and found myself wallowing in self-pity. Then I saw what I was looking for—broccoli crowns and cauliflower heads in white, purple, and gold. Not bathed in beautiful afternoon sunlight the way the pumpkins were, but there they were, ready to be cooked.

On a weekday, the drive is pure pleasure. The countryside is being itself. The point isn't that you've gone out of your way for a head of cauliflower. You've made the trip to show your respect for the person who grew it. It's also a reminder that Plain people aren't just hipsters who take Sunday off.

Even on nights when I come home with nothing, I've gotten something: the view of green and gold farmland out to the horizon and the simple relaxation that comes from driving on quiet, two-lane blacktop. You could call the place paradise, and somebody already has. In that broccoli, those eggs, that pork chop, the countryside has become yours.

Plain Markets

If all you have is a horse, a buggy, and a kick scooter, grocery shopping is tough. And if your kitchen has only a small propane refrigerator, it's even tougher. All the big store chains have hitching posts for horses and buggies, but if you just need some small thing, that's a big deal. The result is what I call Plain markets—local shops that sell the things rural Plain people might need in a pinch.

Like a convenience store, you can buy a Coke or a cup of coffee, but you can also buy sacks of sugar and flour, and all sorts of repackaged bulk groceries at low prices. It all makes sense if you normally cook for ten or twelve people, and for the rest of us, it's a reminder of the days when many people did just that.

Know what you're shopping for. Prices can vary greatly. Sometimes there are bargains, and other times you'll feel like the victim of extortion. What Plain stores often have are obscure items such as locally milled flour and cornmeal.

A few Plain food markets such as Horst's and Kauffman's Fruit Farm cater to visitors too. It doesn't matter if you're a tourist, urban shopper, or somebody coming into the area for work, they'll have both what the locals need and what they hope you'll need. Even if you're in a store that has nothing at all for visitors, don't feel intimidated. Just browse and say hello.

As that old joke goes, if they don't have it, you probably don't need it.

Centerville Bulk Foods

3501 SCENIC ROAD, GORDONVILLE

Centerville Bulk Foods, the place to stock up

It was nearly dark when I started browsing the aisles at Centerville Bulk Foods. Outside, thick fog was on the ground, and clouds were the color of buggy sides. The shop, normally lit only with skylights, was growing dim, so an Amishman fired up a few kerosene lanterns and said, "That should help!" It did. I was suddenly able to read the difference between the flour varieties on the shelves in front of me.

Centerville Bulk Foods is run by Amish staff. It's across the street from a one-room schoolhouse and has more horse-and-buggy parking than just about any other shop in the county. If you're looking for "Amish food," you should know that Amish people don't eat much differently from the rest of us, though they use a higher percentage of homegrown ingredients.

If you have ten or fifteen mouths to feed regularly and entertain a hundred or more guests a few times a year, this is your place. Here you can find bulk sacks of grains and cereals, huge cans of mashed potatoes, gallon-size vanilla extract, 5-pound sacks of erythritol (the sweetener that keto fans adore), six kinds of salt (including Himalayan pink salt and saltpeter), big pieces of inexpensive cheese, so much candy I couldn't look at it, and 50-pound sacks of sugar.

Centerville Bulk Foods could also be a health food store. You can buy whole grains, local fruit, and vitamin supplements. If you're cooking for people with restricted diets, you can do pretty well here.

There are also bulk diapers, bulk plates, bulk everything you need to run a household as long as you have the space to store it. Canning supplies. Jars. Containers. Plastic bags. This is a store for producers more than one for mere consumers. Everything you need to sell at your next farmer's market is here. And if you haven't harvested anything, you can buy bulk pie filling, flour, and shortening and bake up some turnovers.

The store might not have electric lighting, but there are fridges and freezers full of stuff I didn't know you could buy retail: fat-cured salamis that most delis will cut up for you, big bags of burgers, and huge tubs of ice cream—perfect for folks who just spent ten or twelve hot summer hours working in the fields.

The artisanal is on hand too. They offer their own line of unique canned goods such as green cherry tomatoes, carrot relish, pineapple jam, rhubarb jam, red beet jelly, plum jam, and red or yellow sweet pepper jam.

This isn't a big place, and if anything is missing, it's baked goods. That would be competing with their customers. And there's hardly any produce, just a few off-season vegetables and bushel baskets of apples. Centerville doesn't offer the area's widest variety of bulk foods. That honor goes to Shady Maple (page 16) with its basmati rice and whole-wheat couscous—global in reach, but higher prices.

Sometimes I think that if Centerville doesn't have something, it must be too frivolous for me to need. But that's not quite true either. People often want the things this shop doesn't have because they're homesick— think of coarse-ground cornmeal becoming a pot of polenta in an Italian expat kitchen. Nevertheless, the Centerville pattern is simple and satisfying: frugal, local, traditional, useful.

Lancaster Central Market

23 North Market Street, Lancaster
www.centralmarketlancaster.com
Tuesday and Friday, 6 a.m.–4 p.m.; Saturday, 6 a.m.–2 p.m.

On a bitterly cold winter morning, Central Market in Lancaster was a worthwhile destination for one good reason—it is inside a well-heated, red-brick building with decent public restrooms and has a large parking lot. It felt like a good place to spend the rest of the day.

I wasn't the only one to think so; the place was packed. People were buying and eating everything from hot pretzels to apple dumplings and cupcakes. The traditional and the trendy go together here; the Taste of Africa, serving Ugandan chicken and peanut spinach, is next to Stoltzfus Bakery, offering doughnuts, long johns, and fritters. Across the aisle, a Thai stand with four curries and spring rolls caught my eye.

There are plenty of local farmers offering eggs, parsnips, potatoes, radishes, turnips, carrots, and kale. But this is the one local market where meat is a star: not only beef, pork, and lamb, but also rabbit and quail. We Americans once took artisan butchers for granted, and here in Lancaster, they're a treasure. Of course all the meat is local; Lancaster is prime grazing land.

In addition to the butcher offerings, there are perfect reproductions of European classics such as Italian hunter's salamis and Lancaster inventions such as liverwurst made with turkey. Meat curing has an almost cult status in Pennsylvania, and in these aisles, reverence is mandatory.

Pies are all over the place. Savory Cuban empanadas, Pennsylvania Dutch shoofly, raisin, and cream pies. Whoopie pies are not really pies at all. If you don't know the whoopie, it's a large, cake-like sandwich cookie with a creamy filling, and super popular in Lancaster.

Lancaster Central Market has been operating in the same building since 1889, and you can see the evolution as you walk the aisles. The shops with corny Amish joke books and strange textiles take you back to the "Amish Country" tourism era, while stalls boasting organic produce, grass-fed meat, and artisan dairy put you squarely in the modern state of American eating.

Central Market in downtown Lancaster

It's easily explained. Once vendors are established, they can stay for as long as they can survive. When new vendors come in, they are vetted carefully by the standards of the time. In the sixties, that would have been small farmers. In the eighties, tourist stuff and souvenirs. Now it's local artisans that get the nod. And that confers a sort of tenure.

Not long ago, the market was a stronghold of local eccentricities, but tastes change. Pickled tripe is gone and air-dried beef is down to one vendor. Cynics say that hipsters have invaded. Those aren't merely hipsters, though; they're the young inheritors of stands that have been in families for generations. If you're twenty-five and suddenly in charge, you're not going to keep the same old stodgy sign mom and dad put up. The market is alive and evolving.

There are stands with stories that beg to be told. One tiny corner sells ground horseradish and lemonade, its owner often grinding the fresh roots on-site. Another spot sells nothing but celery, its plain white shelves sometimes brimming with hearts and other times bearing only a few lonely plastic bags of stalks.

The market is a microcosm of the county: Amish Country tourist trap meets college town meets gentrifying rust belt meets new immigrant meets middle-America farmland. Lancaster city is both an immigrant and college town. The bohemian crowd showing off their new hair color is from the art school down the block. The vendors at the ethnic stalls are from the many blocks of high-quality row houses that surround the market for at least a mile in every direction. And past those streets of solid brick row houses are the farms, some still in Amish hands and others owned by people who might have chosen to buy their property in the Hudson valley if they had more cash.

The choices are endless. I've enjoyed a Pennsylvania Dutch–style apple fritter washed down with a shot of espresso while shopping for dried beef and free-range turkey. You don't have to go for extremes, though. A doughnut and coffee, some sliced ham, a few pork chops, and a jar of jam will do it most days. A big splurge can get you a porterhouse, an organic turkey, or some paté. It's all there.

Hoover's Farm Market and Greenhouses

30 Erbs Bridge Road, Lititz
www.hooversfarm.com
Closed in winter

Hoover's Farm Market is many things. It is part Plain grocery and part farmers market with a mix of local and trucked-in produce. It's a poultry farm with an egg-laying flock next to the parking lot, a greenhouse with a wide variety of healthy plants, and a postcard-perfect setting. Lancaster County is filled with settings that seem to be auditioning for a country-themed Hollywood production; one look at Hoover's, and you know it would be filmed here.

Hoover's offers the local produce that tourists demand while stocking enough variety to bring locals in for routine shopping: you can buy a stalk of brussels sprouts and a pineapple too.

The chicken pen, a.k.a. range, at Hoover's Farm Market

My one point of contention is the brilliant but absurd practice of making visitors pay to feed the animals that are offered for sale in one form or another. You can buy Hoover's superb free-range eggs, and the range is there on display. A few cents' worth of feed is a great activity for a chicken-loving toddler, and a dozen fresh eggs are an equally great treat for adults. It's just that I don't think you should pay twice.

Laugh for a moment, then buy their eggs, meat, and produce. Those big blocks of butter and cheese might be too large for most of us, but if it's something you need, you're better off buying it here than in a me-gamart. Besides, what big-box store is a ten-minute walk from a working covered bridge (page 70)?

Horst Farm Market

582 READING ROAD, EAST EARL
CLOSED IN WINTER

In Lancaster County, you will rarely find the white pop-up tents with piles of corn or jars of jam that one sees in other rural areas. Instead we have farmers markets—seasonal, indoors, and offering mostly local wares. Horst Farm Market is a perfect example. When the sign in front reads "asparagus," it's as good an indicator as any that winter is over. If it says "cut lettuce," spring is here and farmers are back in the fields.

Horst Farm Market combines seasonal produce with grocery bargains.

Supplementing the local produce are a deli offering inexpensive cold cuts and sandwiches, and a grocery store with staples and bulk items. In its tiny space, Horst serves a huge range of clients. Because it's on Route 625 (page 73), it competes with a scattering of specialty produce stands. It's also the grocery for local Old Order Mennonite households, for whom a trip to Shady Maple (page 16) is a major expedition. In addition, Horst is the local convenience store with a coffee pot that's always at least partially full and house-made snacks by the cash register.

This adds up to a balancing act that's been going on for generations. Serious shoppers can buy sacks of flour or cereal in bulk, people passing through can grab a cup of coffee and a whoopie pie, and tourists will pick up a jar of pickles and some Indian corn. If that's not enough, the staff will make you a sandwich.

One day, when the leaves are gone from the trees, you'll see that the only things Horst has out front are pumpkins. In theory, the owners could bake cookies and make coffee all year long, but they don't. When the butternut squashes and granny smith apples are gone, they close for the season. You'll have to get your coffee someplace else.

Kauffman's Fruit Farm

3097 OLD PHILADELPHIA PIKE, BIRD-IN-HAND
WWW.KAUFFMANSFRUITFARM.COM

The owners of Kauffman's Fruit Farm, that small brick grocery store and farm market in Bird-in-Hand, should be congratulated for keeping the place as it is. Real estate like this begs to be converted into a tourist cliché of monumental dimensions. Instead, they've left it as a grocery shop and outlet for local fruit growers. Out-of-town visitors can buy freshly made doughnuts on summer Saturdays and grab a free sample of their apple cider, but first and foremost, this is a neighborhood grocery.

Why come here? Because it's not on a hard-to-find side road or so big that it will take you twenty minutes to get a shopping cart. You can pull in, buy what you need, and be on your way. Or, you can enjoy browsing.

The store-made products are worth checking out, and in season, baskets of apples, peaches, and pears are well priced. You can choose your own fruit from the big wooden bins out front and get low bulk pricing. Although they sell some of what they grow, much of it goes into their fruit butters. A jar of apple, pear, or pumpkin butter is a wholesome alternative to the more expensive and sugar-laden products we usually buy.

Kauffman's apple orchard. Stop, take a few photos, admire the scenery, and then buy some fruit at their store up the road.

Surrounded by cornfields and Amish farms, Kauffman's Fruit Farm has a great central location. Think if it as a sort of frontier border post. The parking lot is a perfect place to watch buggies go by. To the west lies the city of Lancaster with its urban, college-town charm. To the east is the tourist destination of Intercourse. To the south, Route 30 and shopping outlets. And to the north, the farms that the county is famous for. Wherever you're going, Kauffman's is on the way.

Masonic Village Farm Market and Market View Cafe

310 Eden View Road, Elizabethtown

WWW.MVFARMMARKET.COM

I'd often seen the sprawling grounds of Masonic Village from a distance. The hillside buildings and big lawns seemed enough like a university to warrant no further questions. At the foot of the biggest building, I learned that I was wrong; this is a vast retirement community for Masonic lodge members and their families. The campus was once surrounded by rolling farmland, but now the land is dotted with condos and private homes.

I knew there was a farmers market at one edge of Masonic Village. Astounded by the faux-British complex in front of me, I became even more curious. A farmers market in a facility the size of a small European country had to be worth a visit. It turned out that I had a fifteen-minute drive ahead of me.

And there it was, in an old house that looked like a rural English rural tavern, at a crossroads on the ridge line above the village—above everything else in Lancaster too. Apparently this is the county's highest point.

On the August afternoon I visited, the harvest was well under way and the range of foods impressive. The fruit and vegetables included peaches, apples, pears, garlic, melons, cabbages, beets, turnips, and onions. Some of it was grown right there, other items were local, and some were trucked in. The same was true of the meat. There was beef from the village's own herd, local chicken, and Broadbent ham from Kentucky.

Lancaster's specialty food shops typically have large varieties of canned items, and one that caught my eye was blueberry butter—the first I've seen. The baked goods also had a twist: in addition to the usual whoopie pies, doughnuts, and apple dumplings, they carried savory pies such as potato pea, broccoli, and spinach potato.

On the front porch you'll find Market View Cafe, a snack bar with ice cream, hot dogs, and burgers. Maybe it's not as good a choice as the fresh-fruit slushy machines inside, but it's nice to munch on something while you sit there and enjoy the view.

Sunnyside Pastries

421 WEAVERLAND ROAD, EAST EARL
WWW.SUNNYSIDEPASTRIES.COM

Sunnyside Pastries is a must-stop for anyone looking for a reasonably priced pie. It's in the middle of nowhere and staffed by young women who look like they could be leading ladies in Amish romance novels.

Even though the showroom is small, on a recent day there were fifteen or twenty pies lined up in neat rows. I bought a wrapped half of a shoofly pie, thinking it would make a great cutaway photo, but my discipline was on vacation that day. I sat down at the picnic table out front, grabbed the half pie with my hands, and started eating. The molasses flavor was intense, and the double-texture hit of goo and cake overwhelmed me. Was I supposed to be eating it this way?

The half pie was gone in moments. It took a thorough washing to remove the stickiness that ran from my fingertips to my elbows.

While many people count the wet-bottom shoofly as the classic Lancaster County pie, Montgomery pie also has a following. This is a twist on the classic with lemon juice and buttermilk, giving it a tart accent.

But don't pass up the fruit pies. When you see baskets of peaches, berries, or apples in local markets, there's a good chance fruit pies are on offer too. Save shoofly for winter, when it was meant to be eaten.

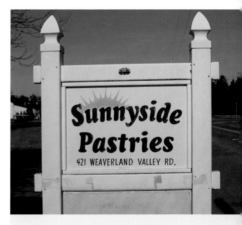

The Sunnyside Pastries shop is behind the barn.

Shoofly pie is so closely identified with the Pennsylvania Dutch that most outsiders have never heard of it. Consisting of cake, molasses, and crust in a pie pan, it's the perfect winter season farm recipe, which is no doubt why it is so iconic. Somebody once told me that anything you put in a pie crust becomes a pie, but what happens if that thing is a cake? It's the sort of question for which you never find an answer.

There are at least three kinds of shoofly. Wet-bottom shoofly pie has a layer of gooey molasses between the lower crust and the cake. A dry-bottom pie is baked longer, so the goo firms up. In theory, chocolate shoofly pie has a layer of chocolate under the molasses, but in practice, the two often combine.

Each shop touts their version as the best. As I made the rounds, it was starting to feel like choosing a wine. I eyed each disk of pie dubiously. Was there a better one down the road?

Allergy Orchard

2600 WILLOW STREET PIKE (ROUTE 272), SUITE 303, WILLOW STREET
WWW.ALLERGYORCHARD.COM

Coping with food allergies is difficult. That's where Allergy Orchard comes in. For people who want to enjoy eating prepared foods yet avoid certain ingredients, this bright and austere shop is the place to come.

Karen, one of the owners, extended her arm across the store like a prize model on a TV game show and said, "Everything here is without something." From the vast array of gluten-free products to tomato-free ketchup, if there's something you can't eat, you can find something here to take its place.

Some people are surprised to see a room filled with processed foods. But these shoppers aren't making the choice between local produce and the supermarket; they're looking for alternative products that won't make them sick.

For those with potentially life-threatening allergies, the Allergy Orchard carries a collection of pins and bracelets that sufferers can wear to inform others in emergencies. Shopping here might not be a point of pride, but knowing where to find tasty, allergy-free foods is a lifesaver for some.

5

GARDENS, PARKS & TRAILS

Climber's Run during early summer. This is about as natural as it gets in Lancaster County.

Climber's Run

226 Frogtown Road, Martic Township, Pequea
www.lancasterconservancy.org
Closed during summer camp hours in July and August

If you're looking for a place to enjoy nature, Climber's Run has it all: a rushing stream, a lily pond, walking trails, a nature center—and plenty of parking.

As you walk up the bank of Climber's Run, remember that "run" is a Pennsylvania word for a stream or brook. With water tumbling over big rocks, mature evergreens, and a steep, wild forest on both sides, you can, for a few moments, imagine yourself in the deep wilderness that's a hundred miles north. Below the brook is the lily pond. If you're an artist, bring your paintbox and easel and see how you stack up against the masters. If you're a naturalist, spend some good-quality time with the wildlife. And if you're just visiting, see if you can spot a frog or sunbathing turtle.

Stop and listen. The sounds here are always a pleasure. Climber's Run rushes along. You hear it in the distance, and when you follow the trails along its banks, it's loud enough to drown out everything else. At the pond, there are chirps and croaks and an occasional splash when a frog dives off a lily pad.

In years past, the land was cleared for farming, but now it's heavily wooded with oaks, maples, and hemlocks. You'll also find wildflowers and native grasses. The Lancaster Conservancy owns and manages the property with an eye toward encouraging native plants and boosting bee pollination.

It's not just about plants. Climber's Run is a classic Pennsylvania trout stream and home to a natural fish population. A fishing license is required, and catch-and-release rules are strictly enforced.

How did this land evolve from farm to forest? The stone house was built for a farm in the 1860s, but apparently the operation didn't go well. The steep hills that surround it and the rushing stream that cuts across it must have made raising crops difficult. By the late 1960s, the land was in the hands of the Boys Clubs (now Boys & Girls Clubs) and called Camp Snyder.

Over the years, land donations and purchases expanded the property to its current 82 acres, while grants and volunteer efforts restored the camp structures and turned the old bank barn into an environmental-education center.

The Nature Center is open by appointment only and draws school groups, many from nearby downtown Lancaster. Climber's Run is a patch of nature at its best.

Tucquan Glen Nature Preserve

800 RIVER ROAD, PEQUEA
WWW.LANCASTERCONSERVANCY.ORG

This corner of the county is on the wild side, with pockets of farmland tucked into steeply rolling hills. Too hilly to be farmed and not populated enough to suburbanize, this region is worth a visit.

Tucquan Glen, a thirty-minute drive from Lancaster City, is perhaps the largest and wildest of the county's wooded landscapes—a deep, forested valley with a stream that tumbles down to the Susquehanna River. Even though it's in as remote a place as exists in Lancaster, you can't miss it. The road for a hundred yards around is a forest of no parking signs. Park in the lot just a bit south and across the street from the trailhead.

If you're not a serious hiker, simply follow the blazes painted on the trees. The yellow ones take you from River Road to the railroad that parallels the Susquehanna. Or hike in a few hundred yards and make a right turn on the white blaze trail, a steep up-and-down loop that returns to the yellow trail. Turn left when they rejoin for a walk that's a total of 2 miles long.

Heavily wooded and with large rock outcroppings, there's a hint of the wilderness you typically see in the northern part of the state, but the earth underfoot isn't mountain; it's the soil of fertile farmland. You won't find any signs of former civilization on these trails. No building foundations, no remains of old barns, not even old heaps of coal or gravel. In that sense, it is a glimpse of what the area was like before it was cleared and developed.

The glen has something to offer all year round. In spring, you'll find wildflowers coming up and leaves budding. During the summer, some parts of the creek are deep enough for a refreshing dip. Fall color breaks out in October. Thanks to the cool air that lingers in the glen, fall comes a bit earlier than it does in the fields a few miles away. During winter, the trails are a pleasant walk if there's no snow on the ground, and a good destination for snowshoeing when there is.

On the south side of the creek, you'll find an abandoned road that takes the same route down to the river as the yellow trail. Because you'll have to ford Tucquan Creek, it's a fine route during dry spells when the water is little more than a trickle, but other times it can be knee deep.

With no cell phone service and a thick layer of forest between you and civilization, you'd best bring a map. Sometimes you can find them in a box by the parking lot, or download one from the Lancaster Conservancy website.

Tucquan Glen is a refreshing change from the rest of the county. The trees, flowing water, clean air, and steep hills offer a wilderness experience. You can't backpack here—there are only a few of miles of trails, and camping is forbidden—but you can revel in nature. It might be all you need.

Trolley Trail

Don't look for signs marking the start of the Trolley Trail; there aren't any. But that doesn't mean nobody knows about it. Indeed, I noticed the parked cars at the River Road trailhead for years before I found out why they were parked there. Like many Lancaster County trails, the ability to walk the Trolley Trail depends more on your luck with parking than your trekking skills.

The Trolley Trail follows a wild section of the former Pequea-to-Lancaster trolley line between River Road and the Colemanville Covered Bridge (page 70). It's clear enough to form a right-of-way and overgrown enough to feel like a woodland. Many walkers will feel more comfortable in boots than sneakers, and in high water, several streams must be crossed on stepping stones. Downed trees aren't cleared with the zeal that they are on routes popular with bicyclists, and there's been enough erosion to leave more than a few exposed roots. This is a wilderness trail that happens to be level.

Park in the pullover on River Road and find the State Game Lands sign, and then the path behind it. You'll know you're in the right place if you're following the river. Even though there are all sorts of paint markings and no-trespassing signs, none mark the Trolley Trail itself. The path follows the Conestoga River and you follow the path—through forest, down a couple of flights of stairs, across two streams—both of which could vanish in dry weather—and along the river rapids. It's placid, hour-long walk.

After a mile and a quarter, the trail ends at an RV turnaround for the campground and the Colemanville Covered Bridge, and you'll have to retrace your steps. The Trolley Trail will be as nice going back as it was coming.

Lancaster Junction Trail

TRAILHEAD PARKING: 99 CHAMP BOULEVARD, MANHEIM

WWW.CO.LANCASTER.PA.US

Lancaster Junction Trail, 2.3 miles each way, is a Lancaster County immersion experience. Unlike the Trolley Trail, the Junction Trail offers a surface smooth enough for strollers, bicycles, and wheelchairs. Add the tree canopy that covers at least 90 percent of the route, and you have a perfect outing for the very young, the very old, and those of us who aren't as fit as we should be. If you're in running shape, it's an easy thirty-minute jog out and back.

Park in the lot just off Route 283. Past the lot and the restrooms, the trail divides the Lancaster County Public Safety Training Center from a

Gardens, Parks & Trails

Pastoral view from Lancaster Junction Trail

farm field. You might expect the trail to quickly become rural, but the sprawling Spooky Nook sports complex occupies one side of the right-of-way for about a quarter mile. Then things quiet down as fields open up. Once you're past the first road crossing, you'll be able to hear the sounds of cows and sheep in the distance.

The scenery varies from farms to forests, with Chiques Creek along one side to keep you company. In one narrow corridor, it looks for a few yards like a wild river.

The Lancaster Junction Trail is never empty. You'll zip by elderly men with a cane in each hand just seconds before a serious runner zips by. On weekdays, groups of retirees stroll and chat while moms wheel their toddlers, stopping every now and then to get them walking. It ends at Lancaster Junction—a warehouse, a cluster of typical rural Pennsylvania homes with inviting porches, a single-track railroad line, and a crossroads. The abandoned railroad grade that made up our trail has become front lawn for a few of the homes.

Since you can't park here—it's someone's yard, after all—you'll have to turn back. Check in with the grazing cows and sheep, see if the corn has grown since you came past, and soak in the pastoral pleasantness.

Lancaster County Central Park

1050 ROCKFORD ROAD, LANCASTER
WWW.CO.LANCASTER.PA.US

SHUTS ENVIRONMENTAL LIBRARY
3 NATURE'S WAY
WWW.LANCASTERLIBRARIES.ORG

LANCASTER ENVIRONMENTAL CENTER
1 NATURE'S WAY
WWW.CO.LANCASTER.PA.US

Kurtz's Mill Covered Bridge, one of the most idyllic spots in Lancaster County Central Park

On a summer day, the first thing you'll notice about Lancaster County Central Park is the happy sound of kids playing in the big public pool. The pool isn't the only appealing thing about this rambling park, but it sets the tone. Park there and stop in at the main office in the house across the road, where you can find out about the wide range of activities here and in parks across the county.

Lancaster Central Park is in the center of Lancaster County, an easy walk from the southern end of downtown Lancaster. It's our biggest park by far and, like New York's Central Park, an urban backyard.

If there's one activity that unites Lancastrians, it's picnicking. If you find an amazing steak or some pork chops at a roadside market, this is the place to fire up a grill. In fact, you'll see people cooking up feasts in the many picnic areas almost every day that weather permits.

The Garden of the Five Senses is down the hill from the pool office. This is a cool place to stroll on a hot summer day. There are mornings when I keep walking past the gardens and buildings and onto the miles of trails. While the terrain is hilly, it's not rocky or difficult. Sometimes you're walking in the woods, and a moment later you're in a meadow, on an abandoned road, passing through Kurtz's Mill Covered Bridge (page 70), or at the edge of a skate park.

Another Central Park gem is the Shuts Environmental Library. Located at the edge of the park in a circa 1769 stone house, the library houses a well-chosen selection of nature books, periodicals, Books on Tape, and videos. Operated by the Department of Parks and Recreation, its circulating materials can be borrowed with a Lancaster County library card. You'll find everything from plant identification guides for small children to philosophical musings on the environment, along with gardening and cooking books. And the garden is the perfect spot for reading.

A few steps away is the Lancaster Environmental Center, offering scheduled activities. You'll find an up-to-date list on their website. From tent camping to the tennis courts, baseball diamonds, soccer fields, and community garden plots, all areas seem to be in constant use. And finally, there's Rock Ford Plantation—a historic house and barn that has its own entry (page 126).

Conewago Recreation Trail

2385 NORTH MARKET STREET, ELIZABETHTOWN
WWW.CO.LANCASTER.PA.US

The Conewago Recreation Trail is a study in contrasts. This pastoral rail trail is a wide, fairly level asphalt or gravel path with shade trees alongside and woods and cornfields on either side. Then there are the sounds. Not far from the main highway between Harrisburg and Lancaster, the noise follows you. And there are days when the roar of aircraft taking off and landing at Harrisburg International Airport adds to the cacophony. If you're the sort of person who brings a soundtrack, put on your headphones and enjoy the best rail trail in the county. If you are seeking out the whispers and songs of nature, you'll have to go elsewhere.

The Lancaster County section is just over 5 miles long, starting outside Elizabethtown and running along the county line to a spot in rural—some might say remote—Mt. Joy Township. Beyond those 5 miles, it leaves the county and continues toward Mt. Gretna and the Cornwall Iron Furnace, ending in downtown Lebanon about 15 miles later.

Lancaster County's rail trails are similar in terrain and scenery, but there are differences in practicality. The Enola Low Grade (page 100) is quite long but is often closed in one place or another. The Lancaster Junction Trail (page 95) is shorter but easy to get to. This trail isn't far from the highway, and there's a bicycle shop with snacks about 2.6 miles from the start. Yes, it's a compromise, and a good one at that. All I suggest is that you bring earbuds.

Warwick-to-Ephrata Rail-Trail

WWW.EPHRATABORO.ORG

When it comes to converting railroad beds to public pathways, some municipalities are more ambitious than others. The Trolley Trail (page 94), for example, is so rough that it would be difficult to navigate on a mountain bike. By comparison, the Warwick-to-Ephrata Rail-Trail is more refined. Running between Lititz and downtown Ephrata, it offers a beautifully paved surface with at least a mile lit for evening use, long stretches of split-rail fencing, mileposts, and even art. It's a masterpiece of a rail trail. Many rail trails are called linear parks, and this one feels truly parklike most of the way. Some of it passes behind suburban

Sign on the Warwick-to-Ephrata Rail-Trail. As you can see, Ephrata's Main Street is about a mile down the path.

backyards. You'll never feel like an interloper, though, since fencing makes the boundaries clear.

Even better, the 8.2-mile route has public transit connections at both ends. Parking at the Ephrata trailhead is on the corner of East Fulton Street and Railroad Avenue. The Warwick/Lititz trailhead begins at North Oak Street between East Main Street and Front Street (about a mile from the center of town via East Main Street), but there is no dedicated parking. However, there is a bus stop with regular service to downtown Lancaster at the corner of Oak and Main.

Enola Low Grade Trail

WWW.ENOLALOWGRADETRAIL.COM

Rail traffic through Lancaster County was so heavy in 1900 that the Pennsylvania Railroad needed a bypass line for express trains. That led to the creation of the Enola Low Grade, a two-track line that turned east from the Susquehanna River just south of Columbia. Then, thanks to the impressive Safe Harbor Trestle, it gradually ascended to a height that could traverse Lancaster's rolling farmland without sharp turns. It crossed the countryside, passing through Quarryville before rejoining the Pennsylvania Main Line in Atglen across the border in Chester County.

During the Pennsylvania Railroad's heyday, the route moved traffic through Lancaster County at great speed. The Enola Low Grade rail line was used for many decades, but when dwindling rail traffic forced its closure, it became a long, straight, flat rail trail. On a bicycle, you can appreciate the easy grading that the line was built for. You can fly here in ways you can't on any other route, sometimes 7 or 8 miles without a break. The eastern end of the trail has a rougher surface, but it's level and almost uninterrupted.

Walkers might see things differently. That vast, carless corridor that beckons strong cyclists may seem boring after thirty minutes or so. And with giant power lines running overhead, it can feel more like a science fiction dystopia than a trail.

In fact, you'll notice these lines and towers before you see signs of the trail. The route also carries electricity from a dam on the Susquehanna

Along the Enola Low Grade Trail. Huge power lines mark the entire route.

River to the Philadelphia Main Line. Those lines power much of the Keystone Corridor rail system. Entrances and parking are located throughout the southern half of the county.

Wolf Sanctuary of Pennsylvania

465 SPEEDWELL FORGE ROAD, LITITZ
WWW.WOLFSANCTUARYPA.ORG

Northwest of Lititz, the spaces between the farms fill with trees, and the lowlands, wet with runoff, become swamps and ponds. Here the Wolf Sanctuary of Pennsylvania, a nonprofit, runs a wolf rescue—a series of vast pens that hold more than fifty animals.

It's been more than a hundred years since wolves roamed the Pennsylvania wilds, and yet they're still with us. Because they're so close and so distant, they're icons of our relationship with nature. Sadly, wolves don't do well in proximity to people, and that's where the Wolf Sanctuary steps in. Animals that are sick, injured, or displaced wind up here.

DNA testing shows that only some of the animals are pure wolf, but they all share classic wolf traits and cannot be returned to their native habitats. Pure wolves raised in captivity can't be taught to survive in the few environments in which wolves still exist, and wolf/dog mixes that were intended as pets can't be returned to their birth homes.

Visitors are always accompanied by a guide, and reservations are required except on weekends. On those days, the gates open a half hour before the guided tour begins, and close when the tour gets underway.

Saturday nights closest to full moon are special occasions, when hundreds of people gather for music, a bonfire, entertainment from an Edgar Allan Poe presenter, and the company of wolves and fellow wolf lovers. It's like a big party.

Go on a Saturday for your first visit. People travel a long way to see the wolves, so be sure to arrive at least a half hour before the scheduled gate opening and expect to park some distance from the visitor center if the crowd is large. Walk down the marked trail to the souvenir shop and ticket building. Once you pay and get your wristband, an expert will give a talk and answer questions. That's when I realized that much of what I thought I knew about wolves was wrong.

Soon the gates were opened and the broad dirt lanes between the pens were filled with people. Guides were stationed in front of many of the pens. It felt like performance art: a continuous stream of wolf knowledge, lore, and the backstory of some of the wolves; the information somehow moved with you even though the speakers stayed put. You might hear about a specific wolf at the top of the hill, something else about the same creature a hundred yards down, and finally see him at the bottom.

Each wolf was seen as an individual with a vivid and unique personality. Their names are never ironic and always literate in some way: Frodo, Sky, Lincoln, Tioga, Lucas . . . serious names for serious animals.

And in fact, each one has a story. The sanctuary doesn't take in wolves from the wild. They all had a previous life as either a pet or a captive. I'm not sure who would want a dog-shaped creature with dinosaur jaws and paws the size of frying pans in their home, and my doubts were confirmed when their histories started emerging. It didn't take much effort to imagine some misguided soul bringing home a wolf or wolf mix, discovering that they are nothing like dogs, and needing to make other arrangements.

The sanctuary is a reminder that wild animals stay wild, even if they occasionally exhibit pet-like behavior. Nature isn't always ready to sleep at our feet.

Conestoga Trail

WWW.LANCASTERHIKINGCLUB.COM/TRAIL-GUIDE

On an afternoon that was cool enough to be bug free and warm enough to be comfortable, I set off on what I took to be the northern terminus of the Conestoga Trail. Orange trail markers and a decayed wooden sign read "Conestoga Trail System," but it didn't take more than a few seconds to realize that the clearly blazed trail wasn't the Conestoga. It was the Horseshoe Trail, which leads east to Valley Forge. The Horseshoe turned into the woods and away from Lancaster County while the Conestoga Trail stayed on the road.

During the next mile, the salmon-colored markers became fainter and the signs smaller. And then, when we turned off the road and into the woods, the trail vanished into a sea of mud. Suddenly the markers were gone and replaced with a "no trespassing" sign.

At 65 miles long and marked sporadically with salmon-colored rectangles on trees, utility poles, guardrails, and signposts, the Conestoga Trail is something of a hiker mystery. Books and websites that cover Pennsylvania footpaths have plenty of nice things to say about it; however, they fail to mention how to find it or stay on it. With only a set of detail-free, downloadable maps for reference, getting lost can become a fait accompli.

In theory, the Conestoga Trail is a footpath from Holtwood to Brickerville, but in practice, it's mostly paint. If you don't mind the roadside walking, you could hike the whole distance in four or five days.

Two parts of the trail are worth exploring. First is the southernmost section, where it travels though a group of nature preserves. You'll find steep ups and downs and woodland peace. Between its start at the Susquehanna River and end in the town of Pequea, the trail winds steeply through the rocky woodlands that run on cliffs above the big river. Another interesting stretch runs through Lancaster County Central Park (page 96). Here you'll find an excellent forest walk followed by a riverside path suitable both for bicycles and wheelchairs.

This park section is worth noting for another reason: you can get there by public transit. A bus from Lancaster city to Willow Street stops at Golf Road, where you enter the park. When you reach Route 462, 5 miles up the trail, another bus will take you back to town. This section begins by crossing a golf course on a paved road and ends with a long walk through suburbia, but in between it's rural.

No matter what route you choose, download the maps from the Lancaster Hiking Club website. They might not have much detail, but they're a start.

Middle Creek Wildlife Refuge

100 MUSEUM ROAD, STEVENS
WWW.PGC.PA.GOV

Middle Creek Wildlife Refuge is a popular place to stroll, hike, or bird-watch. Most of the trails are easy enough for children to enjoy, and the visitor center offers exhibits about the local ecosystem. The refuge surrounds Middle Creek

Migrating snow geese at Middle Creek Wildlife Management Area

Reservoir, a lake built during the 1970s that has done an impressive job of attracting birds and other wildlife—most famously snow geese.

In late February, vast flocks of these white-feathered creatures descend on the lake for a few brief days and feed in the surrounding fields before resuming their long migration.

When the geese are there in full force, the little lake becomes an ocean of birds. On the shore, a dense forest of photographers wait for action with their finest telephoto lenses. For the most part, there's a standoff. The geese pay no attention, until suddenly they take to the air, thousands at a time. They fly in perfect formation, a vast avian spiral that darkens the sky.

Dawn and dusk, when the birds are most active, is also the coldest. There's no friendly coffee shop down the road, so you'll have to remember to bring a hot drink. Expect company, even if you get there before daybreak. The visitor center parking lot is likely to be full, and the shoulders along the park roads will be packed, especially near the trails to the pond.

By the middle of March, the geese are gone and the out-of-town photographers are on to another subject. Middle Creek Wildlife Refuge is once again what it was—a small reservoir with an engaging visitor center and some great nature trails. It's worth a trip anytime.

The National Watch & Clock Museum in the town of Columbia

MUSEUMS & HISTORICAL RE-CREATIONS

National Watch & Clock Museum

514 POPLAR STREET, COLUMBIA
WWW.NAWCC.ORG

You might not expect to see a building this large when you drive up to the National Watch & Clock Museum in Columbia. The wide, low structure resembles a mausoleum (it's a former telephone exchange that's been expanded). Inside, though, you'll find a well-organized, world-class collection.

There's not much in the way of explanation here: no exhibit called "how a wind-up clock works." Rather, the museum showcases a broad collection of timepieces through history. There's a replica stone from Stonehenge, sundials, and other examples of ancient attempts at timekeeping.

An impressive collection of tall clocks features exquisite woodwork and plaintive faces that cry out to you, harkening to the days when a clock was the only device in a household that offered any information at all. I got the answer to a question that's haunted me for years: Why are they called "grandfather clocks" in regular conversation and "tall clocks" in museums? Hint: it has to do with a pop song from the late nineteenth century.

The display of ships' clocks includes a presentation on longitude. Again, the period clocks are amazing. We are shown how longitude was first measured and how precise timepieces made it possible. I'd seen a less impressive exhibit at a similar museum in Greenwich, England. However, throughout the museum, sound effects—ringing chimes, ticking movements, cash register sounds in the jewelry store exhibit—lace the experience with a touch of theme park.

The exhibit on railroad clocks and watches tells the story of how official time zones were created, and contains clocks and watches made in response to the need for coordinated, accurate timekeeping: large, clear faces for train stations—the first public places where people expected punctuality—and tiny, equally clear railroad watches for train crews and station employees. Everybody wanted to be "on time," and a whole industry evolved to make that happen.

During the railroad era, mass production reared its ugly head. Large numbers of identical parts were roughly stamped, then finished and assembled by hand. Soon there were dollar pocket watches, wristwatches, and timepieces with cartoon characters on them.

By the time I got to the modern era, I understood the appeal of watchmaking: the elegance of the engineering, the reason the front dials were called "faces," and the way the faces spoke to those of us who were willing to listen.

The last item on exhibit is everyone's least favorite timepiece: a parking meter. In a museum it seemed even more ominous. Outside its curbside environment, it reminds you of its power.

Don't leave just yet. The gift shop offers insights into the museum's expected visitors. In addition to items such as watch-themed T-shirts and fleece pullovers, there are thick reference books for connoisseurs, clockwork model kits for budding craftsmen, and a cabinet of fine watchmaking tools. I was tempted to try assembling my own timepiece.

LancasterHistory.org

230 NORTH PRESIDENT AVENUE, LANCASTER

WWW.LANCASTERHISTORY.ORG

What was Lancaster like as a British colony? During WWII? Who lived in your house? These are among the thousands of questions addressed at LancasterHistory.org. The facility, called the Campus of History, contains a modest museum, a superb historical library, an arboretum, and Wheatland, the home of President James Buchanan.

Start at the library. Check out the atlases to see when roads were built and what existed alongside them back in the day. My own quiet residential city neighborhood turns out to have once been industrial, and houses that I assumed had been built on farmland were on property that previously held a factory. Open a city directory and find out what was on a particular spot in any given year. Even the notion of Lancaster County as Amish Country has a history.

The small museum opposite the library in the main building has a modest collection of old items. Lancaster was never truly wealthy, and much of the good stuff wound up in Philadelphia. The wax statue of former president James Buchanan almost makes the man look happy. Did he ever smile in real life? You'll find bound volumes of newspapers in German and English, strangely tiny or huge books, and unidentifiable household objects. They are somehow more than their stories, a sort of Lancaster time machine.

Even more evocative is a work table belonging to Thaddeus Stevens. This where Stevens, a senator and Lancaster's historic hero, is said to have done his most important work. Most of us know Stevens as the guy Tommy Lee Jones played in the 2012 movie *Lincoln*. It's easy to imagine the Stevens/Jones character sitting at this table, fiercely penning the Thirteenth Amendment while downing mugs of beer.

You might expect the history of Lancaster to be filled with the stories of the various Plain sects, but they barely figure. Before WWI, nearly everyone here was Plain. Nobody had electricity, and plumbing was rare. Clothes that weren't black or white marked you as a rich urbanite. A dress worn by Harriet Lane, James Buchanan's niece, a major figure in the 1860s fashion world, is on display; the dress is black with a modest white print.

The austere design of two quilts in the auditorium recalls work by artists such as Frank Stella, but these were done decades earlier. Clean and modernist, they were sewn by hand. The lack of decorative frills calls attention to their craftsmanship, and the pattern forces you to wonder how this aesthetic moved from Lancaster quilts to Manhattan art galleries.

Across the grounds is Wheatland, home of James Buchanan, the fifteenth US president. Stevens may have been a bigger hero, but Buchanan had the nicer house. Set in a wooded piece of land with a vast lawn, the 1828 house seems to have been designed by an architect who couldn't decide between the federalist and Greek Revival style. The result is a bit boxy, but inviting in its own way. And those great old trees that cover the

Wheatland, part of Lancaster's Campus of History and the home of President James Buchanan

grounds are collectively known as the Tanger Arboretum. In the middle of the city, it offers a refresher course on the magic of trees.

Like the town as a whole, the tour guides seem ambivalent about Buchanan. The questions that people typically ask don't help things along. "Was the Civil War really his fault?" "Was he gay?" "Didn't he drink a lot?" I won't share the answers.

Buchanan bought Wheatland in 1848 for $6,750, a steep price in those days, but the affluent neighborhood surrounding Wheatland wasn't developed until long after Buchanan passed away.

Buchanan apparently swore off marriage after his fiancé broke off their engagement and died. However, he had custody of a niece and nephew who lived with him at Wheatland. The niece, Harriet Lane, became good friends with Queen Victoria while her uncle was serving as the American ambassador in London, and later acted as first lady when he went to the White House.

Lancaster has always been a tiny bit behind the times, and that may have saved Wheatland from becoming just another fancy home. In her old age, Harriet sold Wheatland to the Wilson family, who occupied it for more than forty years without seeing the need to update it. This created the ideal conditions for a proper restoration. Some years after the Wilsons willed it to the Lancaster Historical Society, it was turned into a museum and opened to the public in October 1937.

Railroad Museum of Pennsylvania

300 GAP ROAD (ROUTE 741), STRASBURG
WWW.RRMUSEUMPA.ORG

If you're serious about trains, Lancaster County is your place, and the Railroad Museum of Pennsylvania is train central. First opened in 1975 with equipment shown at the 1939 New York World's Fair, it has long been a major center for the preservation of trains and train paraphernalia. The exhibits contain the largest and most impeccable collection of vintage railroad gear anywhere. Steam locomotives aren't soot-covered smoke belchers; they're as clean as operating rooms with every part visible. Passenger and freight cars are shown the same way.

There's a chance to imagine yourself shoveling coal in the brutal heat of a steam boiler or loading freight in freezing cold. Passenger cars from various times and places tell stories about what train travel was like for all sorts of people.

Trains have been so important for so long that the museum has restorations of restorations. Ponder a passenger car built in 1886, rebuilt in 1939, and restored in the 1970s. You'll also find a replica of the locomotive known as "John Bull" that was built in the 1930s to display 1830s technology.

Most train museums expect viewers to know the basics, but here their operation is described in detail. My favorite exhibit is the steam locomotive with the controls explained. Having seen images of guys in striped caps and overalls pulling levers and twisting dials, I now have a better idea of what they were dong.

Those hulking machines steal the show, but they're only part of it. The exhibits of tools, uniforms, and dining-car china bring old railroad travel to life. Even the small is big. Those wrenches could weigh 50 pounds; the dinner plates are like lead. Imagine carrying a plate of food to the table while the floor is moving under you at 90 miles an hour.

Work trains are at the back of the big shed. There's a geared Shay steam locomotive for logging, and an executive conference room car—a reminder that railroading was once one of America's largest industries. A rail line that shaved hours off a schedule or reached a mine or mill first could bring a fortune to its backers.

It's not all steam locomotives. Diesel has been around for almost seventy years, and here are examples of the first freight diesel locomotives and the streamliners that made luxury passenger runs. The big reveal is what's inside—those huge engines work on the same principle as modern hybrid automobiles. Who would have guessed?

This stretch of road is so filled with rail activities that it's difficult to tell where the museum begins and ends. The steam locomotives out in the yard are part of the museum, but the steam locomotive belching black smoke across the street belongs to the Strasburg Rail Road (page 116). Also nearby are model train layouts, a motel made out of repurposed cabooses (next entry), and toy train collector shops, all with separate schedules and admission.

A steam locomotive on exhibit outside the
Railroad Museum of Pennsylvania

Red Caboose Motel

312 Paradise Lane, Ronks

Choo Choo Barn
Strasburg Train Shop

226 Gap Road (Route 741), Strasburg
www.choochoobarn.com

There are two subcultures thriving in Lancaster County. Railfans are people who love trains. They'll travel the world to ride—or just watch—particular lines. Then there are model railroaders—people with a passion for building miniature railroads. For them, this is an art form that includes designing not just railroads, but whole landscapes. If you're in either world, you can't do better than to spend a few nights at the Red Caboose Motel . How do you even describe this place? America is filled with freight trains, but they no longer have that iconic piece of equipment—the caboose. They were a train's headquarters, a place where the conductor could sit at a desk and do the paperwork that all that freight demanded. On long-haul trains, cabooses included kitchens and bunks.

The rooms are a cross between a hotel room and a real caboose, where bunk beds and a flat-screen television meet in an authenticity versus amenities draw. This should disappoint only the most extreme fanatics. For the rest of us, the thought of waking up at the crack of dawn surrounded by well-maintained, vintage cabooses is a major thrill.

There's also a dining-car coffee shop, a petting zoo, a buggy ride service that takes in a different part of the county than its competitors, and a tower you can climb for a pastoral view.

Get something from the dining-car coffee shop and sit back. You'll notice the piercing whistles of steam locomotives from the Strasburg Rail Road down the street. On a day when the trains are running frequently, a spot here in front of the motel is the best place to view them. The steam locomotives fly right by and give you one of the very few live opportunities to hear why generations have called them "choo choo trains."

Cabooses at the Caboose Motel. When they say you'll sleep in a real caboose, they mean it.

A strip mall a mile closer to Strasburg deserves serious attention from model railroaders too. It contains a huge layout called the Choo Choo Barn, and next door, the Strasburg Train Shop, a model railroad supplier. Spending time here gives you a sense of the power that building a train layout offers. Here's where you can choose the train equipment, trackside buildings, and the natural environment that your line runs through. It seems frivolous until you start making choices of your own.

Then and there, those of you who like asking the big questions can ponder the underlying purpose of the Red Caboose Motel. Is it a giant model railroad? Or is it meant to be a fun place for railfans and their families? It's both; of course it's both.

Before you go, please remember that the nearby Strasburg Rail Road is for tourists and runs in the middle of the day. Steam locomotives won't wake you up in the morning or put you to sleep at night. They're just down the line, though. In Strasburg, train culture envelops you.

Strasburg Rail Road

301 Gap Road (Route 741, Ronks

www.strasburgrailroad.com

Strolling along the platforms at the Strasburg Rail Road, you can't help but be impressed. The trains are polished! Beautiful passenger cars and hissing steam locomotives wait for you to board. It's quite a thrill. For me, the sight of a steam train chugging through southern Lancaster County farmland is one of the best experiences on offer.

I found myself in a quandary, though: Is riding a steam train better than watching it fly by from a great viewing point? Plus, many of these trains break my rule about tourism in Lancaster County, which is to buy only what you came for. The Strasburg Rail Road is probably the best steam train outing in the state, but offering cheese onboard makes no sense at all. It's a distraction for train lovers, and cheese connoisseurs will do better at Misty Creek Dairy or Central Market (page 79).

For the truly passionate, there's only one activity at Strasburg Rail Road that counts—the shop tour. I wasn't the only one thinking this way. Ten other people gathered at the meeting point—and not just oldsters. Half were under fifty, and our guide Alex told us he was twenty-two. He tried to be a comedian, but his remarkable knowledge kept getting in the way.

As massive steam engines pushed and pulled in the background, we were shown around a shop filled with big metal pieces that spoke of the past. Wheels as tall as adults. Wrenches as long as my arm, followed by wrenches that were even longer. Whereas things are getting smaller in the modern world, from cars to electronic devices, this old-time bigness filled the vast shop.

The steel parts that make up a steam locomotive aren't 3-D printed or made with computerized milling machines. Instead, they're fabricated with the same tools that were used to made the originals a hundred years ago. Big pieces of metal that are kept in one end of the building are pounded, cut, and polished in the traditional way, recalling a time when engineers made horsepower, not technology, and craftsmen with hammers and wrenches defined what was cutting edge.

A "doodle bug" at Strasburg Rail Road

Finally, Alex asked if there were any more questions. Always ready with a question, I asked, "How does a steam locomotive work?" With the most excited expression I'd ever seen on a tour guide, he stepped over to the biggest loco in the building and proceeded to give the clearest explanation of a mechanical device I'd ever heard. I was tempted to ask him to explain a jet engine—another device that baffles me—but I didn't. It would have been pressing my luck.

National Toy Train Museum

300 PARADISE LANE, RONKS
WWW.NTTMUSEUM.ORG

I was blindsided by the emotional charge that toy trains carry. Model railroading has been a father-son activity for generations. It's what we did in the days before video games and robotics competitions. I visited the museum because I was curious about the tiny steam locomotives and came away with an appreciation for other people's fondest memories.

I overheard people talking about their childhood and the grown-ups who shared a love of model trains with them. If you have such memories, this is holy ground. It exudes nostalgia in a way that the big railroad museum up the road doesn't (page 111).

Some of the toy trains are big enough to sit on, while others, such as the tiny Z scale, with its thumb-sized cars, are so small that whole layouts could fit in a briefcase. Anyone have a set of those Lionel trains with the three rails and big, chunky cars, or maybe cheaper plastic boxcars and pressed-metal track? A lucky few will recognize the high-end and hobbyist gear with tiny handbrake wheels, perfectly reproduced locomotive actions, and barely visible rows of rivets.

Each operating model railroad layout is its own universe of tiny villages, drive-in theaters, coal-fired steam locomotives, and plaintive whistles. More than anything, they celebrate a world once ruled by trains—although I spotted a modern Amtrak Superliner like the real one I rode on a few months ago.

With no real emotional connection to model railroading, it felt like I was looking at venerable objects in the temple of a faith I couldn't comprehend. The passion locked up in these carefully rendered scale models is palpable, yet the cultural phenomenon is never described in the way you'd expect from a museum. I left wishing that someone could give me the guided tour.

Ephrata Cloister

632 WEST MAIN STREET, EPHRATA
WWW.EPHRATACLOISTER.ORG

"What is this place?" is a legitimate question when you first catch sight of the Ephrata Cloister. It was once a religious community—some might call it a cult. Now, with restored buildings, and some that are re-created, it's a park that celebrates a founding moment in Pennsylvania's religious history.

Ephrata Cloister in winter

In the 1720s, Conrad Beissel, a Christian spiritualist, left his native Germany to find religious freedom. Like many European immigrants who came here to escape religious persecution, he rejected Roman Catholicism and believed that only consenting adults should be baptized, a practice known as Anabaptism. Indeed, this is the tenet that unites the many Plain sects of Lancaster County.

Soon Beissel had formed a small community, which he named Ephrata, and built a chapel and dormitories for its members. Not many of the original structures survive, but those that do form the core of the museum. The sisters' house, known as the Saron, is the most impressive. When it was constructed in 1743, it was almost certainly one of Pennsylvania's largest buildings.

Life wasn't exactly fun at Ephrata. Beissel believed in celibacy and felt that members could get closer to God by eating and sleeping less. He expected Christ to return at midnight, so members were awakened at that time for a two-hour worship service. When they did sleep, it was on hard wooden bunks with wooden blocks for pillows.

For many, though, life here, with its steady food supply, was better than what they had. The residents were creative and productive. They wrote hymns, printed books, and penned works of classic German calligraphy. In the Pennsylvania of the time, this sort of idealistic extremism was almost taken for granted.

All this sacrifice haunts you as you walk the grounds. Today, the buildings are surrounded by mowed lawns dotted with vegetable gardens and bread ovens. Tour guides explain the community's faith: a form of Christianity that sees God as having both male and female forms.

This is a good place to think your own deep thoughts. On special occasions, local experts demonstrate the cloister's crafts and perform its music, often in the distinctive white robes that the members were believed to wear.

When the cloister closed its doors as a religious institution in 1934, there were still a few people living on the grounds. Today, the faith founded by Conrad Beissel may have left Lancaster County, but two churches remain in Pennsylvania. It's not over yet.

Rough and Tumble Engineers Historical Association

4997 LINCOLN HIGHWAY EAST, KINZERS

WWW.ROUGHANDTUMBLE.ORG

Pulling in to the Rough and Tumble Engineers Museum on the morning of an event can be disconcerting. Don't be afraid to park between two half-ton pickup trucks. Let's be clear, though, Rough and Tumble was made for folks who drive these hefty vehicles.

People say that there's always something going on at Rough and Tumble, but that's not exactly true. It is open two days a month, and only in the warmer months. The woman selling tickets couldn't quite grasp why I couldn't quite grasp the simplicity of this. It explains the crowds though.

An antique tractor pull was scheduled on the day I visited—a Lancastrian twist on that popular farm-country spectacle (see Buck Motorsports Park on page 173 for the real thing). Rough and Tumble offers something for everyone as long as you define "everyone" as being male and over fifty. I was less than happy to notice that this included me. I fit right in with the hundreds of unsupervised older men wandering between the antique tractors, carefully examining their huge tires and enjoying the soundtrack of vintage internal-combustion engines.

Restored tractors lined up at Rough and Tumble Engineers Historical Association

You quickly realize that Rough and Tumble is one of those Lancaster County mash-ups: part museum, part flea market, part motorsports venue, part engineering history club. Cynics might also say part junkyard, but for the regulars, every scrap is a treasure. It's not so much a refuge from modernity as a place where mechanical things have cult status.

After a few hours, you get the feeling that this crowd relishes its obsolescence. Cell phones are few and far between. This isn't loss or deprivation, it's immersion. If you have a secret—or not so secret—love of engine noise, this is the place to indulge it. Nobody puts their fingers in their ears. Nobody tries to scream over the machinery. In an otherworldly way, you are at peace with loud.

Although the facility seemed to be a campus of exhibition buildings, not all were open. While the farm machinery exhibits were open, the buildings devoted to cars and scale models were locked. You are free to look around, and nobody will stop you from trying to converse with the regulars, but choose your conversations carefully. If you're not an expert, don't bluff!

One other group of historically minded people will find Rough and Tumble worth a visit: book collectors. The selection of antique repair manuals and topic-specific books is unequaled. Even if you've seen a 1930s farm machinery logo at some other museum, it's not likely the museum will have an accurate facsimile handbook to flip through and enjoy the graphic design of that era.

A crowd gathered as the antique tractor pull got under way. They cheered and clapped as those pristine old machines dragged a sled loaded with cement blocks. To me, it was less interesting than watching paint dry, but not to the guys around me. If they had to watch paint dry together, they'd discuss antique-pigment chemistry and fondly remember the conversation months later.

Big Spring Farm Days

Swiss Pioneer Preservation Association
735 Spruce Road, New Holland

Big Spring Farm Days is an example of the effort it often takes to find out about Lancaster County's most iconic community events. Check billboards! Check place mats! And check the local paper.

What should you be looking for? "Farm Days" or "Family Days." These are public events meant to put some aspect of traditional life on display. Big Spring Farm Days is the most extreme case of hard-to-find information.

Its sponsor, the Swiss Pioneer Preservation Association, offers no easy way for outsiders to contact it. There seems to be a museum / meeting hall at Big Spring Farm, but it isn't open to the public. All you can do is cultivate your sources.

At the one I attended, I wondered why it attracted so many Old Order Mennonites, and it didn't take long to get an answer. This group can trace its ancestry back to Switzerland, and this is their celebration. There's food, a tractor parade, and craft workshops. The skills on display—everything from harness making to sawyering—seem to be aimed at preserving the way things were done a century ago. Yet, some of the Plain groups are already living something of a nineteenth-century existence. For them, these are shared survival skills; for the rest, it's nostalgia. The antique tools aren't being restored as a hobby; they're meant to work.

If you don't catch this event, similar ones are held throughout the summer. Maybe you'll learn how to use an ax? Make cream cheese from scratch? Spin your own wool? Sometimes you don't even know what you want to know.

Christiana Underground Railroad Center at Historic Zercher's Hotel

11 Green Street, Christiana

WWW.ZERCHERSHOTEL.COM

With the Mason-Dixon Line as its southern boundary, Lancaster County has good reason to claim its place in Civil War history. People often zip though on their way to Gettysburg, and that's a mistake. Our border location allowed local free black families, backed up by Mennonites and Quakers, to play a leading role in the Underground Railroad. Slaves escaping from the South were secretly escorted to the Canadian border, where slavery was abolished in 1833, and no laws called for the return of these freedom seekers.

Of course, that didn't stop a reverse Underground Railroad from forming that kidnapped free blacks and smuggled them down south into slavery Nobody even rumored to be involved could breathe easy.

The Christiana Underground Railroad Center at Historic Zercher's Hotel is devoted to this history. Located in the village of Christiana, not far from Route 41, it's just a room of well-maintained exhibits in a classic nineteenth-century building. On hand are beautiful maps that describe Underground Railroad destinations in Lancaster and Chester Counties. This pre–Civil War–era building is connected to an old factory that has some Underground Railroad history of its own, and a brick corridor links the museum to Zercher's Hotel. On private property behind the hotel is an abandoned stone arch railroad bridge. It sits in the sort of dense woods that passengers on the Underground Railroad must have appreciated. Under the cover of night, escapees could get a modest break from the hidden compartments they traveled in and enjoy a sip of water or a bite of food.

Christiana is historically significant for another reason. It was the site of an uprising in 1851 that many saw as one of the first skirmishes of the Civil War. What happened has been described as the "Christiana Riots," the "Christiana Uprising," and the "Christiana Incident." It unfolded as men searching the area for escaped slaves met with local opposition, and the search party's leader, the slaves' owner, was killed. At least thirty-seven people from the opposition were arrested, and the only one who stood trial was found not guilty within fifteen minutes.

This reverberated painfully though the slave states, a resounding reminder that the North wasn't going to do anything to protect the interests of slave owners. It was called the first battle of the Civil War years before the Civil War officially began. It was a moment of victory for the North, although resistance leader William Parker lost his farm, and his family fled to Canada—via the Underground Railroad, of course.

Two prominent Lancastrians were involved in the aftermath. Congressman Thaddeus Stevens offered an aggressive defense of the resistance, and President James Buchanan (page 109) later tried to keep the nation together. As they say, the rest is history.

American Military Edged Weaponry Museum

3562 OLD PHILADELPHIA PIKE, INTERCOURSE

The American Military Edged Weaponry Museum is the collection of Larry P. Thomas Sr., and like so many passionate collectors, he's ignored his own rules often enough to gather some very interesting material.

It's all crammed into an old bank building in downtown Intercourse, next to Kitchen Kettle Village (page 43). From the French and Indian Wars to the Vietnam era, if it has a blade, it's here.

But there's far more: British weapons, banners, handguns, rifles, machetes, swords, and period books. Bayonets sit next to pikes that are labeled American but look like they're from the twelfth century. As the years roll on, the range expands: handguns, rifles with mounted bayonets, Confederate flags, and then the Stars and Stripes. When we get to the twentieth century, other ephemera sneak in, with two fascinating sub-collections demanding attention.

One collection features cellophane-wrapped cigarette packs, a reminder of a time when everyone smoked. American cigarettes were a currency that could be sold, traded, or gifted anywhere in the world. A soldier could hand a pack to a suffering stranger or to a fellow foreigner among the ruins in places such as Poland or China and make a friend.

Also worth noting is the collection of US Army soldiers' handbooks, introductions to the exotic places where Americans fought, including China and Hawaii. China was known to Americans only through restaurants and laundries in those days. And Hawaii may have had a future as an American state, but nobody knew it then.

The strongest part of the museum focuses on the first half of the twentieth century. Indeed, the world wars vibe was so strong that big-band music was the soundtrack. There were lots of exhibits from the nineteenth century, but no Steven Foster tunes, and plenty of Vietnam without Crosby, Stills & Nash. Swing was the sound of American military greatness.

Rock Ford Plantation

881 ROCKFORD ROAD, LANCASTER

WWW.ROCKFORDPLANTATION.ORG

If you spend some time exploring Lancaster Central Park (page 96), you'll find a big house hidden in its forests. This is Rock Ford Plantation, the home of Edward Hand, a Revolutionary War general and physician. Once the center of a large tract of farmland, it's now in a park, with big lawns, shade trees, and a barn used for weddings and other events.

The house has been beautifully preserved. There are well-disguised electrical outlets and bits of twentieth-century ventilation, but otherwise the decor is faithful to the 1800s. It's not hard to imagine General Hand at home here with his wife and seven children.

Rock Ford Plantation in Lancaster County Central Park

On a grand scale, the rooms don't say much, but when you look closely, a story opens up. Clothes closets have pegs rather than dowels. A table in the elegant dining room, with its bursts of bright color, is set with forks with only two tines. Every diner had what looks like a tiny barbecue fork. When Hand lived here, forks were a new invention, and the design was not quite standardized.

You never went thirsty at Rock Ford. No matter what room you were in, you could have a nip of brandy or a cup of tea. Boxes for storing tea leaves and bottles for distilled spirits are almost everywhere.

Rock Ford Plantation was expected to earn its keep. As a farm, it fed the Hands and their employees; as a house, it showed the wealth and power that a general accumulated. The property also generated revenue as a place for breeding racehorses.

Born in Ireland, General Hand trained as a surgeon and enlisted in the Regiment of Foot, which brought him to Philadelphia in 1767. He traveled to Fort Pitt (today's Pittsburgh) and the Ohio River valley and then back to Philadelphia in 1774. There he married an American, resigned his commission, and started practicing medicine in Lancaster.

When the Revolutionary War broke out, Hand joined the Continental army and was present for George Washington's historic crossing of the Delaware River on Christmas night 1776. In fact, he can be seen in the legendary painting by Emanuel Leutze, holding his hat as Washington led the way.

After the war, Hand returned to Lancaster and took up residence at Rock Ford. He bought the land in several parcels, built the house you see today, and raised his family. In addition to his medical practice, he served in the Pennsylvania Legislature and was a member of the Electoral College that saw George Washington named the first president. He died at Rock Ford in 1802 at age fifty-seven.

Rock Ford still earns its keep by hosting events. Often you'll see a big tent being set up and planners buzzing around. General Hand would have approved.

Hans Herr House

1849 HANS HERR DRIVE, WILLOW STREET

WWW.HANSHERR.ORG

Walking through the orchard at the Hans Herr House takes you back in time. The ripening apples, the vintage buildings, and the mature cornfields in the distance make you dream of an earlier, more bucolic Lancaster.

When Hans Herr built this house in 1719, it was surrounded by the unknown. Native Americans were living nearby and the rest was wild forest. Within a few decades, though, the city of Lancaster was booming. And that's the message: this is where colonial Lancaster began.

Besides the residence itself, the property contains an orchard, several outbuildings, and a Victorian-era home used as a small library and gift shop. Across the street is the Longhouse, a reproduction Native American home of the same place and time as the Herr house.

Like so many historical destinations in Lancaster County, Hans Herr House is a cross between a park and a museum. You can get an in-depth tour or come on a day when the place is closed, and stroll the grounds.

Inside the Hans Herr House you'll find an authentic re-creation of colonial-era frontier life. The scene includes a dining table, hard wooden benches that couldn't possibly have been used for anything other than prayer, and a few tools for working with wood, fiber, and fire. The Herrs had this land, but not much more.

Built in the medieval German style that most of us know only from fairy tales, the Hans Herr House is startling with its height and sloping roof. Even more impressive is the Native American longhouse across the street. We think of Native Americans as living in tents called tipis. A thousand miles west of here, they did. In this area, however, the Susquehannock people embraced what we might think of as an urban lifestyle. A village might have dozens of these structures, each home to thirty or forty people.

Longhouses brought the residents together in vibrant community. Bunks along the side walls and a fire pit in the center evoke the feeling of a giant hiker shelter. But it symbolized home and family. You were related to everybody who lived there, and you knew which other long-houses in the village housed your closest kin.

In contrast to the Herr House across the street, the longhouse is staged with food and clothing. Thanks to the Native Americans' "three sisters" diet of corn, squash, and beans combined with game and fish, the quality of life inside the longhouse was clearly higher than that of the Herr family.

This diet made the Native Americans far bigger and taller than the colonists. A hundred years earlier, Captain John Smith called them "giantlike." That robustness didn't do them much good when push came to shove, however. I want to imagine a time when the European settlers and the Susquehannock natives lived in harmony. But by the time Europeans began to clear farmsteads in central Pennsylvania, most of the Susquehannock population had succumbed to diseases introduced by their European neighbors. The few natives that remained were slaughtered by a local gang called the Paxton Boys, an event so gruesome that even the least sympathetic settlers considered it a crime. It was the story of America told in miniature, though it wasn't what Hans Herr was hoping for when he built this fairy-tale dwelling.

Landis Valley Village and Farm Museum

2451 KISSEL HILL ROAD, LANCASTER
WWW.LANDISVALLEYMUSEUM.ORG

Landis Valley Village and Farm Museum, a few miles north of downtown Lancaster, evokes nineteenth-century village life. A museum village in the most literal sense, its streets were part of the thoroughfare that ran between Lancaster and Reading, and the buildings are positioned as they would have been long ago.

Begun in 1925 as a roadside attraction by two brothers, Henry and George Landis, the museum grew in size and scope when the state acquired it in 1953. On busy days, museum staff in period costume will try to engage imaginary visitors will time-travel comments like "They make forty cents a day and pay twenty cents for room and lodging," or questions like "Have you ever heard of Oprah Winfrey?" It's startling but charming.

An apple pie ready for its top crust at Landis Valley Village and Farm Museum

The well-kept period buildings, shade trees, pastures, and unpaved lanes are equally enchanting in blazing autumn sunshine, a spring drizzle, or a gentle winter snowfall. Those with a deep interest in history can find information on everything from heirloom plants to antique blacksmith tools and heritage-breed cows. In fact, the cows grazing in the village pasture look slightly different than the ones populating local farms. They are from a time long before electric milking machines and lend extra authenticity to the place.

In 1985, the staff began cultivating heirloom-variety seeds. Today you can buy those seeds from several sources, and heirloom garden plants are for sale at the annual Mother's Day Plant Sale. Check the museum website for details.

North Museum of Nature and Science

400 COLLEGE AVENUE, LANCASTER
WWW.NORTHMUSEUM.ORG

I wasn't sure if the North Museum of Nature and Science was for kids or grown-ups. The cheerful women at the front desk offered "Both!" in answer to my question, although the boxes of crayons scattered among the exhibits suggest it skews toward the younger set.

Start with the vast collection of stuffed birds in the basement, displayed in cases so old that they too could be exhibits. Looking at the owls, a whooping crane, and a condor, I could feel the creeps coming on; it could have been a hall in New York's Museum of Natural History circa 1961. The elegant glass displays were held together with wood that had seen the elbows of generations of engrossed families.

In addition to a mineral collection, the basement contains a case of ancient Egyptian objects. You can see something far more impressive in a big-city museum, but that's not the point. Those Egyptian objects are a reminder of old Lancaster; they were donated by locals who traveled there in the days before export controls on historic artifacts and weight restrictions stopped travelers from bringing such things home.

Main entrance to the North Museum of Nature and Science in Lancaster city

If you ignore the crayons, this is what all museums were like before they became entertainment venues. When you're ready to experience the museum as entertainment, head up to the main floor to view a science-project rocket, small live animals, plaster casts of dinosaur bones, and interactive displays—things that parents hope will make their offspring smarter.

There's also an art gallery and a planetarium, which has a modest dome and a presenter with whom you can chat after the show—something you can't easily do at, say, the Hayden Planetarium at New York City's American Museum of Natural History.

In a nutshell, the basement is for inquisitive adults, and the main floor is for kids. The family could take in the planetarium show all together too. Not bad for a small-town museum.

Demuth Museum

120 East King Street, Lancaster

WWW.DEMUTH.ORG

If you've been to the big art museums in New York or taken a college-level art history class, you'll know at least one or two paintings by Charles Demuth. He was in Paris with the Lost Generation and in New York City with the modernists. Like many creatives, Demuth marketed his art in the big city, but when it was time to head into the studio, he returned to Lancaster, where he painted some of his greatest works.

Demuth had a solid vision, strong technique, and knack for networking. Georgia O'Keeffe was a frequent visitor, staying in a downtown hotel. William Carlos Williams wrote the poem that inspired Demuth's legendary painting *I Saw the Figure Five in Gold*, and Alfred Stieglitz, John Marin, and Gertrude Stein also popped up in his life.

Even if you don't know much modern art, you're probably familiar with *Figure Five*, which features a big number five and radiating geometric shapes. Walking over to the museum after a cup of coffee at Square One (page 32), I was thinking so hard about this painting that I forgot its home is in Manhattan. Is it cubist? Modernist? Both?

I'd hoped to find a deep and enlightening collection of work by Lancaster's favorite artist, but only six of his works were on display. However, photos of Demuth's home and family provided some insight into his personal and professional lives. In the self-portrait on the second floor, he looks deep and frail, nothing like the entertainer he was said to be. But that may be a disguise. Perhaps he painted it thinking, "I'll look like a genius in this one!" In that case, the joke is on us.

Demuth was related to the family that owns the oldest tobacco shop in America, Demuth's Tobacco Shop. It's next door to the museum at 114 East King Street and is open occasionally for tours and souvenir shopping.

7

ANTIQUES, AUCTIONS, COLLECTIBLES & UNUSUAL SHOPS

Houses at Stoudtburg Village, a Bavarian-style
residential enclave

Stoudtburg Village

1 NORTH MARKET STREET,
REINHOLDS

Stoudt's Black Angus Antiques Mall

2800 NORTH READING ROAD,
ADAMSTOWN
WWW.STOUDTS.COM

Well, how did this get here? Stoudtburg Village is a fairy-tale "Bavarian" town where people actually live. The brainchild of the owners of the restaurant, brewery, and antiques mall next door, it was an attempt to add character to a town already brimming with it. This whimsical village contains single-family residences with European-style facades and American-style garages, a condo community with theme park overtones, shops, and a town square with a fountain and cherub statue. Stroll through and enjoy the effort that someone expended to create an Old World vibe. Some say it's corny, but that's part of the appeal. Dreams are free, and you're free to walk this phantasmagorical simulation of a European town center and imagine anything you want.

A stone's throw away is Stoudt's Antiques Mall (a.k.a. Stoudts Black Angus Antique Mall). This sprawl of windowless buildings is the largest single antique vendor complex anywhere. It stretches on forever, one structure leading into another. This expansiveness isn't just about the variety of vendors, but the stature of some of the offbeat pieces themselves: manor-sized tables, mirrors, beds, and apothecary cabinets. Rugs that cover a room, paintings that cover a wall. I fell for the portraits. Maybe, like me, you're looking for a great ancestor to celebrate. You could buy a 4-foot-wide portrait of a noble-looking person and hang it in your living room, then throw a party and challenge your friends to invent a biography about the subject. Bring home a hefty piece of wood furniture and pretend it's a remarkable family heirloom.

None of this comes cheap, but you could easily spend more in an upscale furniture store. And besides, the life and personality of these pieces add another kind of value, a chance to create continuity and tradition in your life.

You won't go hungry, either. Attached to the antiques mall is one of the oldest microbreweries in the region, as well as a bakery selling egg sandwiches on homemade breads, plus whole loaves, pastries, and pizza. There is also a lively bar/restaurant on the main square of Stoudtburg Village, along with a coffee shop that's open on weekends.

There are antiques malls everywhere now, but Adamstown was the first. True fans can spend days here, seeing things that you might have thought existed only on *Antiques Roadshow*. This meandering temple of stuff can be overwhelming to all but the most focused. Even worse, philosophical types may find themselves adrift in an ocean of yesteryear's material culture. Enter at your own risk.

Riehl's Quilts and Crafts

247 East Eby Road, Leola

Countryside Roadstand

2966 Stumptown Road, Ronks

Where do those tourist buses go? You see them on the roads between New Holland and Intercourse and know that they can't just be cruising. They have to stop somewhere, and that somewhere had better have snacks, restrooms, and shopping. Two places come to mind: Riehl's Quilts and Crafts, and Countryside Roadstand.

Riehl's Quilts and Crafts is on an industrious farm complete with a cow barn, wood shop, and fields of crops. Make sure you visit the livestock and check out the garage full of buggies. It's not an exhibit—they're the transportation for this huge household. One might be pressed into service while you're trying to understand how the turn signals work.

Some people call Riehl's and Countryside Roadstand tourist traps, but there are finds if you shop carefully. I'd been in Riehl's half a dozen times before I noticed a rack of handmade men's leather belts. I almost never covet an article of clothing, but that belt reached out to me. Of course, quilts are the big-ticket item among Pennsylvania Dutch artisans. Even at farm shops they often command prices upward of $1,000. This is a serious investment and requires time and effort to get right.

Riehl's Quilts farm shop. Located on a perfect farm, it's simultaneously authentic and over-the-top touristy.

Several miles away, Countryside Roadstand, in Ronks, is a great place to buy jars of preserved fruits and vegetables or locally made baked goods. But the biggest surprise is the large book section. They have many of the same titles as the Mennonite Information Center (page 180), including that mysterious category—cookbooks with deliberately misspelled titles. "Kountry Kookin" seems to be a favorite phrase.

Both Riehl's and Countryside offer huge selections of birdhouses. It seems to me that birds are fully capable of building their own residences. Indeed, even in my urban neighborhood they take the liberty of building them everywhere—on tree branches, in chimneys, and on porches and eaves. It's tough to imagine why human effort is needed to supplement this, but birdhouses are a big deal.

Just as offbeat are the quilted checkbook covers, "quillows," and other quilt-motif objects that crowd these shops. On the other hand, the baskets and wooden toys make appealing gifts. The prices are low, and sometimes it's just nice to leave the main road.

What else? I haven't mentioned my favorite Amish tourist store item: brooms. A handmade straw broom might be a tiny bit too hipster. Or it could be just what you need.

Angry, Young and Poor

356 WEST ORANGE STREET, LANCASTER
WWW.ANGRYYOUNGANDPOOR.COM

People are always looking for a time machine when they come to Lancaster—a perfectly preserved slice of the past that will transport them to what they imagine was a more innocent era. If they can't get innocent, they'll settle for a time when they were happier about facing the future. Angry, Young and Poor fails in the innocence department but delivers in spades on the rest.

Step through the door and into the time when Ronald Reagan was just elected president. You can still buy those T-shirts with foul language that proved you were a rebel. On the wall are 1980s posters that parody 1950s advertising. If, like me, you lived in New York City during the 1970s, Angry, Young and Poor recalls a time when brutal and exuberant became one.

Urban storefront of Angry, Young and Poor

Had it been called Angry, Old and Poor, I'd have visited years ago. And had I done so, I'd have come face to face with the obvious—a store that's been in business for a quarter century can't really call itself "young" in that rebellious rock-and-roll sense, just as the original punk rock fans can no longer be described as "young" either.

On a recent visit, two guys were wearing the black leather, black jeans, and asymmetrically cut hair that once screamed their musical tastes to the world. I first thought they might be in period costume like the presenters at Ephrata Cloister (page 119). Lancaster is the kind of place where subcultures can thrive without much attention from the outside world.

Young or old, you can find recorded music from this seminal era of rock history. The rack of vinyl albums isn't the only one in Lancaster, it's just that the others are more about the medium than the message. You'll also find clothing—maybe "wardrobe" is a better word—for the punk lifestyle, including a fine selection of kids' sizes (minus the curse words, thankfully). According to my calculations, if you saw Sid Vicious live in New York, you're just the right age to have grandchildren who will love this stuff.

If you came of age in the seventies, Angry, Young and Poor will instantly remind you of where you stood on disco. If your blood boils at the very mention of the word, you have to come here. If you didn't get it then, you won't now. Yes, the store made me feel nostalgic for the days when the Sex Pistols seemed new and fresh.

If this is your music, then this is your time machine. There was music after Woodstock and before hip-hop, and it still lives in this corner storefront.

Where were you in 1979?

Country Housewares

589 MUSSER SCHOOL ROAD, LEOLA

White Horse Dry Goods

5426 OLD PHILADELPHIA PIKE, GAP

ALSO CHECK OUT FISHER'S HOUSEWARES AND FABRICS IN GEORGETOWN (PAGE 39)

You can't get her out of your mind. She's that woman in a black bonnet and shawl walking along the edge of a barren, windswept field on a bitterly cold day. All you can see besides that woman as you drive along are white specs of flying snow. Had she not been Amish, she'd have gotten in her SUV to run her errand, turned on the heat, and cranked up the stereo. Instead, she was a film noir image of premature death staring you in the face. You're not in a movie—it's nothing more than an Amish woman heading to the store, one that carries basic items for a basic life.

Five minutes later, you're both at the register. You're buying a 16-quart stock pot and a butcher knife, and she's got a spool of black thread and a Bible story coloring book. You questioned the wisdom of going out in this weather, but for her, it's just another day.

No electricity from power lines, no power tools, and no driving are rules that aren't just tolerated, they're embraced. It's key to an identity that has kept them going for centuries. And there's a retail network to support this life of faith.

I've been developing an eye. Socks are often the first thing you see. Not in brilliant colors or cute, kid-friendly prints, but black socks in every size and thickness. And white briefs for men and boys to go with the black socks.

During my early visits to these stores, I was impressed by the number of children's books for sale. Soon I began to notice their Christian themes, and finally, the absence of dinosaurs. Apparently the Amish don't do dinosaurs. And I'm always amazed by the large selection of Amish romance novels. This is roughly like discovering that cowboys love reading westerns or police officers enjoy detective stories.

Here you can also find oversized utilitarian household objects such as cooking pots and laundry baskets. In this world, cooking for twelve is all in a day's work, and a wedding or funeral that feeds a hundred or more is routine enough to require many plates.

For those of us used to shopping malls, these places are dimly lit. There are skylights and sometimes lanterns, and in the shadows you'll find interesting home-lighting choices. Candles, flashlights in many styles and colors, battery-powered headlamps, and even illuminated tweezers. Plain living means the constant negotiation of darkness and light.

It also means making most of your own clothes. Bolts in the simple, bold colors of Amish dresses and the subtle prints that their spiritual cousins, the Old Order Mennonites, wear are enough to call a department fully stocked.

Besides socks and textiles, you'll find hats, bonnets, jackets, and plain black shoes. They might seem austere, but they simplify getting dressed in the morning.

Esh's Handmade Quilts & Crafts

3829 Old Philadelphia Pike, Gordonville

Country Lane Quilts

221 South Groffdale Road, Leola

Esh's Handmade Quilts & Crafts is Amish owned and targets tourists. But you won't find romance novels, whoopie pies, or candles here. Virtually everything on sale is hand-done needlework. Anna Esh, the owner, is energetic and outspoken. I've been in quilt shops that have more inventory, but Esh's has variety, from the older style that she calls "dark" to bright and modern. When I asked whether the darker quilts came from the colors of Amish clothing, and pointed at her own dress, she told me that Amish people no longer wear out their clothes. Instead, when they're well worn but still usable, the clothing is donated to charities. This has allowed the craft to modernize and adapt.

Esh's Handmade Quilts

Country Lane Quilts in Leola is harder to find. The only clue is a small sign pointing to a dirt road. Follow it to a postcard-perfect farm, where a card in the window says "Open."

Unless you're quick, you will likely be intercepted by the family dog—undoubtedly the friendliest in Lancaster County. Once you're properly welcomed and every square inch of your exposed skin is thoroughly licked, Katie, the proprietor, and her quilts will be waiting for you.

When I asked who makes the quilts, she explained that although her four daughters were "born sewers," most of her inventory comes from independent craftspeople.

Both Katie and Esh mentioned that the quilt business peaked in 2014 and has been steadily dropping off. The reason, they suspected, is that people no longer appreciate fine handmade things. It could simply be that today's young people prefer minimalism to shabby chic, but I kept that thought to myself.

These quilt shops might thrill you, or they might leave you scratching your head. Either way, they're an opportunity to see Plain craftsmanship and passion in the eyes of their owners. You can't find your dream quilt without looking.

Country Knives

4134 OLD PHILADELPHIA PIKE, INTERCOURSE
WWW.COUNTRYKNIVES.COM

I'd heard that Country Knives was a great place to buy high-quality nail clippers and get my knives sharpened too. When I walked in, the first thing I noticed was a long, shiny sword that could have been in a pirate movie. It could have beheaded a buffalo, and it left me frightened. On the other hand, here was proof that they know how to sharpen a blade.

From the street, Country Knives looks like a private home. Only the sign out front and small parking lot give it away. Close to the door are historic swords often used in theater productions; exploring further, you'll find grooming supplies, kitchen knives, pocketknives, and hunting knives.

What you would never do here is ask if they have something. You know they do: Japanese knives for soba, straight razors for barbers, sharpeners for clipper blades, the nail clippers themselves, collectors' miniatures, and the sorts of big blades that survivalists are said to carry. There are Swedish stainless-steel vegetable peelers too.

The staff makes it clear that knives are tools, not weapons, although the most-spectacular knives in the shop were indeed weapons. A staff member also reminded me that a dull knife is far more dangerous than a sharp one. Even though I'd heard that a million times, I bought a new honing steel just to be safe.

Naturally, I had to ask what they didn't have. The answer was switchblades, which are illegal in Pennsylvania. They don't carry electric knife sharpeners either. Recalling the damage done to several of my favorite knives, I nodded in agreement.

You may have heard that ax throwing is a rapidly growing sport. If so, this is the place to buy a proper throwing hatchet. The store attracts knife collectors too; displays show several kinds of blades in dozens of different handles. It supports my theory that if somebody makes something, someone else will want to collect it.

Before I visited Country Knives, I never contemplated the role that knives played in my life. But looking at the displays, I remembered the peeler from grandma's kitchen, the wooden-handle folding knife used for foraging in the Italian Alps, and my very first chef's knife. In a kitchen, in a barber shop, or in a hunting cabin, you need a knife. This is the place to get one. And if you need to get your nail clippers sharpened, they can do that too.

Cornfields Antiques

245 GRISTMILL ROAD, NEW HOLLAND

Cornfields Antiques, as you might expect, is in the middle of nowhere. On a gray day, the open fields and austere farm buildings around it can seem like a set from a horror film. But when the corn is tall and the sun is shining, it's an inviting source for all kinds of treasures. Outside are piles of barnwood along with reclaimed doors and windows—some in sizes that haven't been made in decades. All this stuff is neatly arranged so that there's no feeling of a junkyard. It's a nice place.

Inside, the offerings show signs of passionate curating and a sense of humor. In addition to enamelware and small furniture pieces, there are books and music. The first title I noticed was *Women and Vodka*, which I took to be a memoir. Instead it was an anthology of Russian classics by authors including Anton Chekhov. I spotted another book called *Malpractice*. Was it a medical

Recycled wood at Cornfield's Antiques

thriller? A courtroom drama? A textbook? I was entranced by all this stuff in one place.

Cornfields is nothing if not eclectic. Fascinating books sit just a few feet from bins of old keys. A quilt section in an upstairs nook seemed to thumb its nose at all those "serious" quilt shops (page 141). There was even a charming quilt for less than $100. Its random patchwork and coarse stitching screamed amateur. There was no pattern or apparent craftsmanship, yet it had a unique beauty. Leaving it was like leaving an elderly aunt. I knew I had to go, but I couldn't say goodbye.

If you're serious about antiques, Cornfields is, in many ways, a better destination than an antiques mall in town. It is well curated, and there is no wandering and no space wasted. You might not find what you're looking for, but at least you know that the management has put its best foot forward.

Village Harness Shop

3578 WEST NEWPORT ROAD, RONKS (INTERCOURSE VILLAGE)

When you rely on horses for work and transportation, you need the right hardware to harness the animals' power—items such as bridles, bits, lines, and harnesses made of metal and leather, and often crafted by hand. The Village Harness Shop in the middle of Intercourse (page 43), across from Kitchen Kettle Village, sells serious, esoteric tack for the smallest pony to the biggest Belgian. It manages to stick to its mission while waves of T-shirt-seeking tourists pass by. I was so baffled by the inventory that I returned with an expert.

What I got was a lesson in horsemanship—literally, the line of communication between man and animal. While a horse can hear you when you call out to it from the seat of a buggy, you need something more persuasive to help you along.

The store may be Amish owned, but it isn't just for the Amish. There are saddles and lassos and fancy blankets. And all those grooming gadgets aren't just about showing off the horse. Good-quality brushes prevent grit from building up between the horse and harness and causing pain.

The repair workshop in the back is bigger than the store itself. It's a reminder that the products sold here are meant to be taken care of. With expert attention, a saddle can last for generations. Not everything is made locally, but the staff knows their products inside and out.

Most of us won't ever need to buy anything from the Village Harness Shop. But it's a memorable snapshot of the inner workings of a singular way of life.

Village Harness Shop in Intercourse

E. Braun Farm Tables

3561 OLD PHILADELPHIA PIKE, INTERCOURSE
WWW.BRAUNFARMTABLES.COM

Amish furniture stores are all over the place. Some sell secondhand pieces, and a few, such as Stoltzfus Antique Furniture in Georgetown (page 39), have the solid, useful items that collectors and enthusiasts seek out. There are also lots of small shops producing reproduction Swiss German designs and selling them at modest prices. This isn't so different from quilt shopping; you'll dismiss most of what you'll see, and then suddenly something will turn your head.

One-of-a-kind tables and cabinets made from old wood are an established part of the high-end furniture world in the county, and E. Braun Farm Tables, with a showroom in Intercourse, is one of the most visible makers. The Braun team takes recycling seriously, starting with their shop. Originally a tobacco warehouse, it has solid wood floors that harmonize with the pieces on display.

The furniture is made from barnwood. This isn't a euphemism, but wood taken from carefully dismantled buildings, and it is remarkably strong.

Aged textures, deep finishes, and solid dimensions speak to the practicality of generations of Pennsylvanians. It's like a patchwork quilt, made from something that served a purpose, sometimes for generations.

Many Amish furniture stores proudly display candy-colored Adirondack chairs. Here those classic American designs are reimagined in hideous shades of bubble-gum pink, chrome yellow, and swimming-pool blue. I couldn't stop thinking that they'll become the Popluxe of 2050. Imagine how your parents and grandparents would feel if they saw the prices that midcentury chrome and Formica kitchen tables go for today.

Peaceful Valley Amish Furniture

3347 OLD PHILADELPHIA PIKE, RONKS
WWW.PEACEFULVALLEYFURNITURE.COM

A few miles down the road, I pulled over at Peaceful Valley Furniture on Route 340 west of Intercourse (there is another store at 421 Hartman Bridge Road in Strasburg). After browsing for a while, I saw that they sold things besides colorful chairs.

They know their audience. Many of the goods are meant for the homes of people who go hunting and who entertain their grandchildren. The material is solid wood. The style is similar to what regular stores sold a few decades ago. I bought myself a TV stand.

You can't ignore the wall decor. Paintings of bear and elk, and so many signs! Some were small enough to rest in a modest nook, and others were so big they could cover a wall. One read "Let's Cuddle"; another said "Be still & know that I am God." Many more signs were about grandma and declared that

Chairs on display at Peaceful Valley Furniture

cookies, hugs, or kisses were on hand. Had there been a sign that said "Welcome! Grouchy Old Man Here," I would have bought it.

These stores offer the practical and aspirational rolled into one. It might not be your style, but here and there, a few bits of Lancaster won't hurt.

Shaker Shoppe

616 OWL HILL ROAD, LITITZ
WWW.SHAKERSHOPPE.COM

Some people rave about Amish furniture. They'll mention the sleek designs, top-quality woods, and elegant finishes. When you press them for details, however, it turns out that they're thinking of Shaker furniture, the refined designs first made by the nearly extinct religious sect from New England.

Amish and Shaker furniture might seem like the same genre. They're not, but you can find high-quality Shaker pieces in Lititz (page 45). From the outside, the Shaker Shoppe looks like a fancy bed-and-breakfast inn with a beautiful home in front and a small garden next to the parking lot. Inside you'll find the lean and unadorned furniture that collectors have treasured for more than a century. The furniture in classic Shaker patterns is made in a workshop behind the showroom, which is like a museum, only with pieces you can touch.

Shaker design is said to be a vision of a stripped-down yet elegant future. Look at a dresser and imagine that its shapes and angles may have inspired today's skyscrapers. A chair's austere legs and back foreshadowed today's streamlined look, and perhaps modernity itself.

What they don't have at the Shaker Shoppe is any trace of Pennsylvania Dutch. No wall signs with cute slogans, no jars of pickled beets, and nothing that could be described as a souvenir of Lancaster County. People come here for the furniture. It's well made and loyal to its roots, and you'll pay far less than you would at an equivalent place in New York or New England.

Is this what many people are really looking for when they visit Amish furniture stores? I'm not sure, but if Shaker is what you seek, the Shaker Shoppe is the place to visit.

Farmersville Auction

33 NORTH FARMERSVILLE ROAD, EPHRATA

WWW.FARMERSVILLEAUCTION.COM

On the first October morning cold enough to warrant gloves, I headed out to the Farmersville Auction, south of Ephrata. I bought a cup of coffee for less than a dollar and sat down in the main auction room. The event began with the sale of eggs and cartons of doughnuts. Boxes containing several dozen doughnuts were selling to contented-looking customers for two or three dollars.

At Farmersville Auction, the formerly coveted and once welcomed are offered up to the highest bidder in a place where the bids aren't all that high. It's all out on display in the hope that someone will raise a hand, show their number, and place a bid.

A small glimpse of the stuff you can bid on at Farmersville Auction

7

The few lots of doughnuts were punctuated by pairs of size 10 work boots and followed by cakes, lamps, and ceramic figurines. With that, I realized that Farmersville Auction was yet another source of inexpensive food, clothing, and furniture—an outpost of Lancaster's alternative economy.

The auction has another role too. It's the magic spot where junk can become valuable. Old military uniforms, cast-iron baking pans, or toys pulled from somebody's attic get a bump in value. The dollar-a-dozen doughnuts might be treat for a Plain family with nine children, but a set of prewar enamel pots that goes for five big ones can wind up selling in a Long Island antique store for ten times that amount.

I had a painful moment while sifting through the piles waiting to be auctioned. As I picked up a cheap plastic model train track and locomotive, I started to snicker. But then an alarm bell went off deep in my memory. This was the same HO train gear I dreamed of at age eight—the very thing I had wanted more than anything.

Browse long enough, and you'll see that what's really here are the remains of our lives—odds and ends that aren't good enough to keep and are too good to throw in the trash. Regular watchers of *American Pickers* will recognize the business model. This is hard-core rural Pennsylvania despite the smattering of out-of-state license plates.

Head over on a Tuesday morning. The moment you enter the grounds, you hear the singsong voice of the auctioneer. There were couches in the backroom, boxes of household goods outside, and heaps of smaller objects described as "collectibles" in the main building. And so much kitchen stuff—plates and pots that looked like they'd seen a few sales before. I wanted to know the story of these objects. Who ate from these plates? Who sat on that couch? And who wore those clothes? Most of the books seemed to be hymnals or cookbooks—Lancaster's two obsessions, God and eating, on display.

There are three auctioneers—one at a podium in the main room, a second on a rolling cart that's pushed from lot to lot among the smaller objects, and a third one outdoors, riding on the back of a golf cart between rows of farm machinery and other large items.

While you can get a sense of the place in fifteen minutes, you'll have to stand around for hours to buy something. If you're game, arrive early, note what you want, and stay focused. A television, dining-room table, or wedding gown could be yours. Or not—there will always be someone bidding against you.

Leola Produce Auction

I am in a slow-moving mob of thirty or so people. The crowd follows the auctioneer from corn to watermelon to cantaloupe, all being sold in that peculiar farm-country quantity of too much for a roadside market and too little to interest the big chains. I'm at Leola Produce Auction, where local farmers bring their best fruits and vegetables. If you're looking for large quantities for preserving, catering, or even reselling, this is the place to go.

You might think an operation like this starts at the crack of dawn, but it doesn't. Start times range from 8:00 to 9:30 a.m., not so city boys like me can wake up at a reasonable hour, but so farm families can get their fresh-picked produce to market.

As the mob moves from the big bins to stacks of smaller boxes, the variety of food grows. The auctioneer tells you the quantity you're bidding on—a flat, a case, or a whole cart, while a Mennonite woman with a clipboard records every transaction. While I had my nose deep in a tray of fragrant heirloom tomatoes, a man with a number and a pocketknife picked one up and took a bite. Was he sampling or grabbing lunch? He was gone before I could ask.

Watermelons at Leola Produce Auction. Sample, anyone?

Beefsteak tomatoes, plum tomatoes, purple eggplants, brown eggplants, yellow and green string beans, raspberries, peaches, nectarines, cucumbers, okra, zucchinis, butternut squash, and every color of bell pepper—all were neatly packed and waiting for the woman with the clipboard to mark them sold. All that work, all that food, for ten or twenty or fifty bucks. That's farming.

As the morning wore on and the sun beat down on the big metal shed, people begin to eat: fried egg sandwiches, hot dogs, doughnuts, burgers, and fries. A tween girl was reading an Amish romance novel near clusters of Amish girls who were the subjects of those books. She was eating too.

Leola Produce Auction is perhaps the most perfect off-the-beaten-track destination in Lancaster County. It's an open window on local farmers and their crops, and people are happy to talk to you. But to really appreciate it, you need to grab a number and a fried egg sandwich and start bidding. A week later, when your case of cucumbers becomes a dozen jars of home-canned pickles, the bounty of Leola will hit home.

Green Dragon Farmers Market & Auction

955 NORTH STATE STREET, EPHRATA
WWW.GREENDRAGONMARKET.COM

Root's Country Market & Auction

705 GRAYSTONE ROAD, MANHEIM
WWW.ROOTSMARKET.COM

I spent more than two hours wandering Green Dragon before I realized that the hundreds of vendors sprawling across the grounds sold only certain kinds of things. Cheap sunglasses, socks, jars of pickles, and brightly colored leggings were abundant, along with soft pretzels, subs, ice cream, barbecue sandwiches, and candy. Did I mention socks? There were dress socks, athletic socks, and socks for diabetics. I didn't need any of them though. I needed superglue to reattach a handle to my driver's-side car door, but adhesives were not to be found.

Soon, I refocused my search and found something I never knew existed: a toilet lamp that fit inside the lip of the bowl. This is also a good place to find one of those novelty baseball caps that boast of past military service, number of grandchildren, or your favorite sports team. Pan pudding

VINTAGE · JEWERLY

🔨 TOOLS 🔧

MY AUNT MARY'S PASTA SAUCE

PAMPERED CHEF

GREG HARTING'S SPORTS MEM.
ANTIQUES & TATTED CRAFTS

GUITARS & MORE

Mobil eyez · PRESCRIPTION EYEWEAR

Signs can help you find your way around Green Dragon.

and ring bologna are staple foods, and heavy metal and Christian pop are featured music genres. Shopping at these markets, you can get the feeling that every material thing is at your fingertips, without seeing anything you might want.

Root's and Green Dragon are open on different days and are about 20 miles apart, but they offer essentially the same experience: a vast mash-up of flea market, livestock auction, antique sellers, and food vendors, with a few home improvement contractors sprinkled in. Although they both claim to be farmers markets, don't come just for that. You'll do better at a small farm shop. What you will find, though, are the best flea market deals for hundreds of miles around.

Seize the moment, especially when it comes to food. Norma's Pizza at Root's had received national attention, but I visited the stand three times before I found her open, and had to wait almost an hour for food (she has since closed). On a previous visit, I had had a great falafel sandwich and wanted to share another with my wife, who loves Middle Eastern food. We searched the place top to bottom. It wasn't closed; it was gone.

These two destinations are best visited during the off-season, on a day that's warm enough for outdoor vendors to set up but not so hot that the not air-conditioned metal buildings are uncomfortable. During spring evenings, strings of lights hang over baskets of produce that look far better than supermarket fare and are cheaper than at upscale markets.

One evening while I was loading my car under the glow of parking-lot lighting, a family unlocked their nearby SUV. The were having trouble packing up, and discussing it intently. I looked over and saw that the children were holding some live geese by the feet. They wanted to put the birds on their laps for the ride home, but Mom was having none of it. She made it clear that geese were not pets, and was not about to clean up after them.

I was left squirming. If I'd seen this in a parking lot on the other side of the world, I could have photographed it for *National Geographic*, but this was 6 miles from my home. It challenged my ideas about life, love, food, death, and family.

Mud Sales

Every spring, after the snow starts melting and before the fields are planted, fire departments hold huge fundraisers called mud sales. Once you go, the reason for the name becomes obvious: much of your time is spent standing in soggy fields. Mud sales usually start on a Friday and run through Saturday afternoon. If it's sunny and warm, there's no better outdoor activity in Lancaster County.

Portable toilets portend the crowd size at a mud sale.

Mud sale fans advise you to get there early, but you can never be early enough. Get there at 5:55 a.m. for the 6:00 a.m. presale breakfast, and you'll stand in a long line. Arrive an hour later, and you'll have to park miles away and wait for a school bus shuttle.

The quilt auctions are the high point, but people also bid vigorously for cases of potato chips or secondhand screwdrivers. Mud sales vary. Some have flea markets offering inexpensive tools and clothing—even estate jewelry—while others focus on livestock, buggies, or farm machinery. It's startling to see rows of Amish buggies lined up for auction. Sometimes ten, sometimes twenty, always more than you've ever seen in once place, and with that, the chance to examine them up close. Check out the disk brakes, strangely Victorian upholstery, and generators for safety lighting.

Food is an important element of the mud sale universe, from a big breakfast of eggs, pancakes, and sausage to soft pretzels, barbecued chicken, and homemade chicken corn soup. Oyster stew shows up occasionally, a reminder that oysters were once a staple. No matter what time it is, you'll find doughnuts and cold drinks.

In the auction areas, a sense of calm pervades even as high-priced items raise the stakes and folks stand in the cold spring mud. Mud sales, some in distant corners, give you the chance to see the different parts of the county up close. They're some of the best places to mingle with rural residents.

People start showing up for mud sales at the crack of dawn.

The following fire companies organize mud sales. Dates vary from year to year and are posted on their websites before Presidents' Day weekend.

Bart Township Fire Company
11 Furnace Road, Quarryville
www.bart51.com

Bird-in-Hand Volunteer Fire Company
313 Enterprise Drive,
Bird-in-Hand
www.birdinhandauction.com

Farmersville Volunteer Fire Company
74 East Farmersville Road,
Ephrata
www.farmersvillefire.com

Fivepointville Fire Company
1087 Dry Tavern Road, Denver
www.fivepointvillefire.net

Gap Fire Company
802 Pequea Avenue, Gap
www.gapfire.org

Gordonville Fire Company
Old Leacock Road, Gordonville
www.43fireems.com

Kinzer Volunteer Fire Company
3521 Lincoln Highway East
(Route 30), Kinzer
www.kinzerfire.com

Penryn Volunteer Fire Company
1441 North Penryn Road,
Manheim
www.penrynfire.com

Rawlinsville Volunteer Fire Company
33 Martic Heights Drive,
Holtwood
www.rvfd58.com

Refton Volunteer Fire Company
99 Church Street, Refton
www.refton59fire.com

Robert Fulton Volunteer Fire Company
2271 Robert Fulton Highway,
Peach Bottom
www.513rffc.com

Strasburg Fire Company
203 Franklin Street, Strasburg
www.strasburgfire.com

West Earl Fire Company
14 School Lane Avenue,
Brownstown
www.westearlfire.org

Weaverland Valley Fire Company
403 North Earl Street, Terre Hill
www.weaverlandvalleyfire.com

New Holland Sales Stables

101 WEST FULTON STREET, NEW HOLLAND

New Holland is a wholesale livestock auction, a pivot point where farmers from all over the East bring their horses, ponies, pigs, sheep, and goats to sell—some as pets, some for pleasure, others for work or meat. Before a recent visit, I'd been hearing about the increasing demand for goat meat and lamb and was curious about where the animals come from. But first, I stopped at the snack bar. Desperately wanting to feel like a local, I ordered a scrapple and egg sandwich. Soon I found myself with a group of bearded, sixty-something men and realized I fit right in.

"I came here for the rabbits!" said a guy nearby. I was getting ready to tell him that rabbits were auctioned at Root's (page 152) when somebody asked if he was looking for grass-fed rabbits. "No," he replied. "They have to be carrot-fed if I'm going to bid on them." Then I understood he was joking, but to me, it sounded almost plausible.

I headed over to the bull-and-steer ring, where a digital screen kept pace with the action. What I didn't understand were the two-digit prices these fine animals were fetching. One healthy-looking steer went for "77." I asked Mr. Grass-Fed Rabbit what it meant. If I could buy an animal like that for $77, there would be T-bones for everyone. "It's the price per hundred pounds," he said. That steer was the price of my first three cars combined, not including the auctioneer's fee.

When I found the smaller-animal auction, I found the urban crowd I had been tipped off about. Guys with fancy shoes were bidding on lambs and goats. I took a seat on the wooden bleachers burnished by decades of farmers' backsides and did my best to follow the action.

The Monday horse auction attracts a particularly large crowd of buyers looking for everything from high-quality carriage horses to saddle horses, therapeutic horses, camp horses, show horses, and cart-pulling ponies tame enough for children to drive. Even if you're not in the market for a stylish ride or a starter herd of sheep, New Holland Sales Stables is worth a visit as a place of serious business, a microcosm of the livestock universe.

8

THEATER & ENTERTAINMENT

Rock Lititz Pod 2

201 ROCK LITITZ BOULEVARD, LITITZ
WWW.ROCKLITITZ.COM

Rock Lititz is home to a cluster of companies that serve the music industry. Most people in the area know it as the immense, windowless black box where the world's top performers can hone their shows. For the entertainment industry, it's an off-the-beaten-track facility where acts can rehearse on a private, arena-size stage.

Some parts of Pod 2, the building across the street, are open to the public. It houses the offices of companies that cater to the music industry with instrument services, lighting, and other operations. Non-music-related businesses lease space too, such as a yoga school, a bicycle shop, and a medical practice.

If you think of the music business as a backstage concert fantasy, a visit to Pod 2 will quickly cure you of that notion. The place has the quiet seriousness of a large bank. Entertainment is a global enterprise, and this is its technical center.

Park in the Pod 2 lot and head to the lobby. There you'll find a coffee bar, lunch counter, and microbrewery with plenty of seating. In fact, it's a decent place to take a coffee break if you're

Rock Lititz, one of Lancaster's most unusual and global companies

driving along Route 501. The most interesting thing here isn't a show, shop, or exhibit, it's the tasteful, businesslike feeling that permeates everything. This group of people understands not only that the show must go on, but how it happens. You can feel their focus in the air. It's a reminder than while Lancaster is a great place to visit, it's also a great place to work.

Early Music at St. James Episcopal Church

119 North Duke Street, Lancaster
www.saintjameslancaster.org
Four or five times a year

Elegant, historic, and intellectual, Early Music at St. James Episcopal Church isn't what most people expect from Lancaster. But for hard-core early-music fans, it's what puts Lancaster on the map. What's on offer is pre-1600s European music, coming before baroque, classical, Romantic, and modern. It represents the oldest examples of written Western scores.

St. James Church is an ideal venue for such a performance. From the outside, the church calls to mind a medieval cloister, and inside it's a mix of European cathedral with great acoustics and spotlit theater.

The $20 admission is a bargain for classical music, and if you chat with other audience members, you'll find that many of these passionate fans have traveled a great distance to be there.

We should also note what's not here. Unlike almost every other classical venue in the region, there's no effort to make the music "accessible." No buffet or free champagne with the conductor. Unless you met at music school, this isn't a good spot for a first date. It's not that there's no explaining. Musicians offer spoken introductions, and the program notes go into great detail. Some knowledge is assumed, though.

When the performers take the stage, not only will you hear music that's unfamiliar to most people, you'll see instruments that are the ancestors of what we know. In this church, with its wooden pews in booths and ornate wall decor, you can get a good feeling of what the music was like when it was first played. You have to listen carefully; the projected sound of the modern era wasn't even imagined when these pieces were written. No matter how passionate the score, it is pretty quiet.

Today, music reaches out and grabs us. There's the rock band with its amps turned up to 11. The symphony orchestra with over a hundred musicians playing at once, and when we encounter music on our many electronic screens, it's often backed by bright lights and costumes that are as loud as the sound. None of this happens at St. James. Here, your job is to listen. No matter how hard you try, early music can't be cranked up. Embrace it and appreciate the rare musicians who choose to play these scores.

It doesn't always happen, but sometimes you'll have a listening experience from another time and place. You listen without your mind wandering, and your understanding of music grows. The harpsichords, clavichords, and assorted viols are masterpieces, and during intermission you can examine them up close. You can't do that at Carnegie Hall.

Wolf Museum of Music & Art

423 WEST CHESTNUT STREET, LANCASTER
WWW.WOLFMUSEUM.NET

The Wolf Museum of Music & Art is a brooding surprise. Most days it sits in well-maintained silence on one of the city's more distinguished residential streets. But a few times a year, a "Recital Today" sign beckons on the sidewalk.

On concert days, you have your choice of folding or easy chairs. The last time I went, I took the easy chair and a steel spring popped out of the bottom as I sat down. As the musicians took their turns at the pair of Knabe grand pianos, I sank deeper and deeper into my seat. Luckily, the music was pleasant, because it was a quite a task for me to get up.

At the Wolf Museum, look for a smaller sign that says "Recital Today" or "Concert Today."

This isn't a serious venue for classical music, but a well-preserved home and studio where generations of Lancastrians learned music in the days before schools offered band and orchestra. They came to the house, studied under Dr. and Mrs. Wolf, and gave recitals in the same place they're offered now. When you're seated 10 feet away from someone struggling to get through a piece that's tougher than they thought, you can feel their pain and appreciate their effort.

Maybe you'll simply pass the Wolf Museum on the Lancaster Walking Tour (page 35) and admire the elegant corner house. But when the "Recital Today" sign is out, stop in, find yourself a chair, and immerse yourself in a slice of old Lancaster.

Lancaster Symphony Orchestra Open Rehearsals at Fulton Theater

12 NORTH PRINCE STREET, LANCASTER
WWW.THEFULTON.ORG
WWW.LANCASTERSYMPHONY.ORG

It was on my first visit to the Fulton Theater that I learned an important Lancaster lesson: always wave back when someone waves at you. That day, it was a smiling woman with five or six children. They seemed happy to see me, so I assumed they were making a mistake, and ignored them. It turned out that they were my music-loving neighbors, the sort of people who bring their children to the best free cultural event in Lancaster—an open rehearsal of the Lancaster Symphony Orchestra.

Anybody who's ever wondered how the ocean of musicians that constitutes a symphony orchestra can manage to play both in time and in tune with each other will find a rehearsal fascinating. Open rehearsals are held on Friday afternoon five times a year and begin with a Q&A session with a featured guest artist or orchestra member. I watched as the musicians came onstage. Soon, one of them began giving a talk. He described the role of the cello. It was a bit basic, and then I took another look at those children and realized that this was a good music education moment.

The tone of the talk may have been elementary, but it was welcoming too. A symphony orchestra can be intimidating at close range, and the

Fulton Theater marquee. There's almost always a show going on.

members were clearly doing their best to overcome that. As the music began, the collective energy that makes it special was on display.

As the rehearsal continued, the conductor, Stephen Gunzenhauser, would stop and gently correct the musicians, making sure that they were all together. Watching, you'll quickly notice that this is where the expression "all on the same page" comes from. Each instrument does something different, and yet somehow they all do it together.

There's been a theater on this site since the Civil War era. Over the years it's been a stage for great talent and a venue for B movies, burlesque shows (community outrage shut it down quickly), and vaudeville acts. The big change came in 1995, when the theater became a nonprofit foundation with a commitment to the arts, and the Fulton was restored to its former grandeur.

From the outside, Fulton Theater looks like it should be much bigger than it is. But because the place is small, most of the seats are good. Could seeing a Broadway play here be a better experience than seeing it on

Broadway? No matter where you sit, you are close to the performers. You see the sweat on their faces and the sweep of the stage all at once. Yes, the Fulton is a theater in the classic sense of the word.

It took some time to get used to being this close to something I typically saw from much farther away. I was drawn in, though. And then, it was over. Not for the musicians—they had to stay for more rehearsing—but we fans had to leave. I strolled over to a coffee shop and streamed the very same music over my phone while I was walking. It wasn't the same.

Zoetropolis Cinema

112 NORTH WATER STREET, LANCASTER
(717) 874-0526
WWW.ZOETROPOLIS.COM

For many years, Zoetropolis Art House was a small alternative movie theater hidden in an uptown loft. Finding it was a challenge. You had to go down a hall and up a back elevator, and then through another hall. You arrived in an industrial space with raw brick walls, a modest snack bar, and seating consisting of couches and cushions. The theater seats in the back were for late arrivals, and that could even include people who got there on time but had to make a trip to the restroom and got lost trying to find it.

The movies were college town staples—collections of short films, socially conscious documentaries, and whatever else falls under that category called "art." It attracted a loyal following.

It couldn't stay that way forever. The Zoetropolis Cinema Still House now resides on Water Street in the heart of downtown. It consists of three bars, a Mexican restaurant, and a theater with industrial decor. You can still watch movies sitting on a couch or the old theater seats, or at one of the tables. On my first visit I ordered beer and a pretzel, and the woman who sold me my movie ticket brought the order to my screen-side table.

This is modern Lancaster, offering artisan whiskey, independent films, and even a live stage. On my last visit, there were more people drinking than watching the movie. The bar sells 5-ounce glasses of good beer for three bucks. It's an act of menu genius. Go, have a great time, and make sure to take a cab home.

The evening is just beginning at the Zoetropolis complex.

A twilight Barnstormers home game

SPECTATOR SPORTS

Lancaster Barnstormers Baseball

CLIPPER MAGAZINE STADIUM
650 NORTH PRINCE STREET, LANCASTER
WWW.LANCASTERBARNSTORMERS.COM

In May you start to notice the signs. They're red and they'll say something like "Game Tonight." The game is baseball, and this is the sort of minor-league contest that American legends are made of. A night at Clipper Magazine Stadium is part sports, part entertainment, and profound in its own way.

The Lancaster Barnstormers play in the Freedom Division of the unaffiliated Atlantic League of Professional Baseball. Although the Barnstormers are a recent development, serious baseball has been played in Lancaster for more than 150 years. The first team was named, aptly enough, the Lancaster Lancasters. Among other teams, the Lancaster Red Roses played for years in a smaller stadium near Manheim.

Lancaster was without a professional baseball team for a few decades until the city built Clipper Stadium and, with that, brought in a new team. It went so well that the league made its headquarters here. And for good reason. On any clear summer game night, you'll see crowds of people dressed in team gear making their way toward the stadium.

Entertainment at a recent home game included a trivia contest, a huge American flag paraded around the grounds, a foot race for people dressed as pork chops, teenagers throwing T-shirts into the stands, and more than thirty kinds of local beer, each discussed in detail by those waiting in the long food-and-drink lines.

It was a festival of foul balls and stolen bases. There was none of the exuberance of Little League and little of the skill you see at a major-league game. Batters would often pause after they made base hits, as if to think, "Did I hit it? I don't believe it!" In fact, it seemed like more balls were hit backward into the stands than out into the field.

It's Lancaster, and the crowd is trusting. People leave their coats and bags at their seats when they go for yet another beer or across the aisle to chat with neighbors. Everyone here has something in common—a love of these funky, small-stadium baseball games, with their endless foul balls and innings so short that commercials are shown between them. The scores are wild too. The Barnstormers won a game 14–5 recently.

The announcer kept trying to work the crowd up, which occasionally created a dissonance between the cheering and the action. Players would be standing with their arms at their sides waiting for a pitch while the speakers would boom "Let's Get Loud!!"

According to the large number of people who didn't want to come with me, this was supposed to be boring. It wasn't. You'd watch some amazing combination of a pop foul and two stolen bases followed by an ad for Lancaster Bible College or a local insurance broker. The between-inning antics were fun, and it was a pleasure to be there.

By the top of the sixth, I had blown fifteen bucks on beer and Lancaster was winning 13–2. I thought of leaving but was filled with the fear of missing out. What if Lancaster lost in a breathtaking trio of late-game grand slams? That would certainly be one of the most remembered games in city history, and I wouldn't have seen it. I would have never forgiven myself.

I resolved to stay to the end and not drink another drop. I kept both promises. The opposing team from nearby York scored a few more runs, but not enough to change the story. I wasn't a superfan, but I enjoyed the postgame fireworks that continued as I strolled home. With that, I had to agree with many baseball fans that the minor-league game is the real game. There was entertainment, sports, community, and good beer: Lancaster city at its best.

Bicycle Racing

WWW.USACYCLING.ORG/EVENTS

At least once a month during spring, summer, and fall, the police close off roads, crowds gather, and mechanics diligently adjust some of the snazziest bicycles you've ever seen. This is no club ride. These are serious athletes with big aspirations. Like the players on the field during a Barnstormers baseball game, the best riders at these races have their sights set on professional careers.

Here's a rough summary: Competitors are ranked by their results in sanctioned races. As they earn more points, they become eligible to compete in bigger events. Those with the highest rankings have a shot at professional races in Europe and the sorts of earnings that come with major-league stardom.

No sport has been tainted by cheating the way bicycle racing has. When the riders whiz by, I scream and cheer and just hope they're not doping. Floyd Landis haunts every race in the region.

Let's face it, no discussion of bicycle racing in Lancaster County can avoid mention of Landis, a local boy who won the 2006 Tour de France and was stripped of his win after testing positive for banned substances. He then became a hero in another way, by blowing the whistle on Lance Armstrong. You won't see Floyd at races around here. These days, he's living in Colorado and is in the cannabis business.

Lancaster County hosts three big bicycle races each spring: the Turkey Hill Classic, a road race in the countryside south of town; the Smoketown Airport Criterium, held on an airport runway; and the Race Avenue Criterium, held on the streets around Franklin & Marshall College near downtown Lancaster. There are more events in summer and fall; a quick search of the website will provide specifics.

Bicycle racing on the roads of Lancaster County

If you're a serious fan, claim your spot early. People stake out roadside zones as if they were getting ready for a parade. If that's your game, you can bring folding chairs, picnic coolers, and, along the more rural roads, an entire picnic.

Be careful out there! Bicycle racing is almost as risky for the spectators as the athletes. Stay off the course and be aware of how sharply the zooming bikes take corners. If an official tells you to move, do so—they can see hazards you haven't thought of. I once positioned myself and my fancy camera gear in what looked like a beautiful open spot. It turned out to be where the riders threw their empty water bottles.

There is plenty of fast, but it's not just about fast. It's fun to observe the riders' tactics: racers trying to pass, riding in each other's drafts, and generally trying to avoid crashes. Winning can be about crossing the finish line first or having the fastest average time over a series of events. The guy who came in fifth and did just well enough to be promoted to a more professional category might be the biggest winner. Watch to see if somebody in the middle gets a bigger cheer than the leader.

While some groups, such as the Masters (for racers over age forty-five), are racing for the fun of it, the big events are preludes to professional sports careers. When things don't go well, you can see it on their faces: the crushing disappointment of losing, the pain of a stress injury, or the burn of hitting the pavement at 30 miles an hour.

The strongest riders here will go up a category and become the weaker riders there. The pattern will repeat itself until they reach the top. The next time you watch the Tour de France, notice those guys in the back of the pack. They were all once local stars.

Lancaster Polo Club

FORNEY FIELD
70 CHURCH STREET, ROTHSVILLE
WWW.LANCASTERPOLO.ORG

People are often surprised to hear that polo is played in Lancaster. But with all the horses around, it's simply to be expected. Pick a nice summer Sunday and head over to Forney Field, not far from Lititz, the home of the Lancaster Polo Club. In the Hamptons or Palm Beach, polo matches may be an exclusive upper-crust activity, but not in Lancaster. Even if you don't own a polo pony, you'll feel at home at these matches.

At the field, a few people look like they could be from the Hamptons, but there are many more who seem to be enjoying the fantasy. Mostly though, people come here to tailgate and bring their own alcohol. Without question, the Lancaster Polo Club is the county's premier public adult picnic, and the game—like hockey on horseback—is the background entertainment.

Members have their own parking spots reserved with nameplates. It's a terrific icebreaker. If you feel like chatting, just check out their name plate and ask if they're Mr. So-and-So.

There's even a soundtrack. Elton John was followed by doo-wop when I first settled in. These tunes made me scratch my head for a moment. This was cocktail lounge music! And then I noticed that what looked like a park shed kiosk was in fact a full bar. Perfect for the hundred or so people who were treating this spot as a pleasant outdoor lounge.

Being a food writer at heart, I wanted to know what people were eating. It turned out to be nothing special: hot dogs, chips, pretzels, and those sweet baked goods you see around here. A few kicked it up with fresh fruits, cheeses, fancy crackers, and bread that required slicing. These seemed to be chosen for an afternoon of drinking.

In a way, this is just another get-the-ball-to-the-goal field game. However, unlike football, rugby, or soccer, you're riding a "pony." They aren't ponies, though; they're horses that look just a bit smaller than those you see at rodeos or horse shows.

Lancaster Polo Club in action

It may seem like the players and their horses are in a different universe from the fans, but there's nothing to stop you from wandering down and visiting with them. One piece of advice: the horses might not enjoy attention from strangers. Always ask handlers if you can approach and touch their steed.

I was struck by the players' age range. Some looked like they'd retired long ago, while others could have been entering junior high. Lancaster polo is egalitarian in that sense. Not many people have the skills to play, but it looks like everybody who can play, does.

When you see the mounted players in that classic pose, charging down the field with their mallets raised and trying to hit that tiny ball, you might feel a twinge of excitement. You've seen the iconic image on television, on shirts, and in movies to convey that the people watching are truly upper crust. Now you're seeing it with your own eyes.

Buck Motorsports Park

900 LANCASTER PIKE, QUARRYVILLE
WWW.BUCKMOTORSPORTS.COM

Buck Motorsports Park is the yang to the yin of Lancaster County's peaceful fields. That could be why it thrives. You come when you've had enough of green farmland and pastoral covered bridges. You come for the noise, mud, and mess; big wheels, robust engines, bright lights. It's a form of rebellion.

Driving down, I wondered how many Plain people would be in the audience. Do those who reject automobiles take perverse pleasure in watching powerful engines in action? Or maybe there's some basic thrill in experiencing for a few hours the kind of noise many New Yorkers try to get away from.

If you go, I offer a warning: stop at a pharmacy and buy yourself some earplugs. On one visit, I measured the roar of a pulling tractor at 88 decibels—louder than some airports, not to mention everyone screaming in excitement.

The gates open at 5:00 p.m. and the action starts at 7:00. If you show up early, you'll find the place eerily quiet. So quiet that you can

Tractor pulling at the Buck

understand the words on the country music soundtrack. These are some very sad people singing the blues.

A half hour before starting time, the stands were full, the mood upbeat; the sound of engines revving in the background built the anticipation. As I suspected, there were plenty of Plain people there with big smiles on their faces and trays of burgers and fries on their laps. All of us were here together on a summer Saturday night.

What exactly goes on? Most nights, it's tractor pulling. Tractors take turns seeing how far they can pull a giant steel-and-cement weight called a "sled." While there are other events too, such as demolition derby, the tractor pull is the big draw.

At 7:00 p.m. sharp, the national anthem was sung and the tractors lined up. Streamlined, supercharged, and belching smoke, they were nothing like the friendly-looking machines you see in farm fields.

Purpose-built for pulling and putting on a show, the tractors were nevertheless represented by manufacturers such as John Deere and Lancaster's own Case and New Holland brands. Was this the farm equivalent of stock car racing? Like stock cars, the tractors' resemblance to everyday farm equipment is just noticeable enough to make fans smile.

When the pulling started, the sounds blasted through the stands and the audience went wild, even though all that power couldn't move the sled more than a few hundred feet at a time. The tractors kept lining up on this patch of dirt, awaiting their turn to move the sled.

For regulars, Buck Motorsports Park offers a loud, larger-than-life sporting event, a chance to socialize, and cheap food. It's oddly relaxing, and not a bad way to spend Saturday night if you live on a quiet road 10 miles from the nearest gas pump. It's Lancaster's answer to too much tranquility.

Dutchland Rollers Roller Derby

OVERLOOK ACTIVITIES CENTER
301 GOLF DRIVE, LANCASTER
WWW.DUTCHLANDROLLERS.COM

To the uninitiated, whatever you might expect from a Roller Derby competition, it won't be what you thought. But I can promise you'll be entertained. I have seen the most-urbane cynics screaming for their team without having a clue who was winning. Watching the game, a question arises: Does everyone know the rules? My guess is no, given how often the officials blow their whistles. It helps to know that the sport came from the same cultural stewpot as professional wrestling and Ninja Warrior competitions.

Roller Derby fans can be divided into two groups. The first group sees it as a modern, ironic, and vaguely feminist sports activity popular among young women. For the second group, it recalls the cat fight on wheels they saw on a black-and-white television in 1959.

Roller Derby is a relic of the days when all kinds of live entertainment was on offer. Before you could watch Major League Baseball on TV, you could go to a local arena and see people skate around a track, pick fights with each other, and have a winner declared under some arcane system of rules.

Here's what goes down. Everybody—players and referees alike—have ironic nicknames. Acid Reign and Blackout Betty played on my most recent visit. Are these *noms du guerre* or cute stage names? And each player has a number that seems to have been taken from a telephone area code; one is 717 (Lancaster), another 580 (Oklahoma).

The players line up for introductions. As their names are called, they step forward and offer a raised-hand salute while the crowd cheers. Then the action begins. The skaters move slowly around the track in a big mob, then one from each team zips away from the pack, and after that, the members of the big pack try to tackle each other. Many go down. Later, you'll see them on the sidelines with ice packs. Nursing your wounds isn't a euphemism at Roller Derby. After a tackle or two, the play will stop, the referees (their slogan is "to eject and serve") will confer, and it will all start again.

Dutchland Rollers

It's like short-track speed skating combined with rugby, only the athletes are wearing heavy makeup. Haven't you ever wished that in the midst of the Olympic-level solemnity that surrounds short track, a brawl would break out? Or that instead of the Ivy League seriousness of a women's rugby game, the players showed up wearing metalhead makeup?

That brings up more questions. Is this a parody of something or a fusion of ideas you just can't pinpoint? Did a bunch of punk rockers sit down with a group of cross-dressers and declare "we need a competitive sport that combines our aesthetics! It should be on roller skates! Yes! Let's do it and make sure there's fun stuff for children too!"

As with ballet or NASCAR, you begin to notice details. What does that star or stripe on someone's helmet mean? Do the players known as "jammers" and "blockers" have roles other than trying to knock each other down? The rules of the game might not become obvious, but you can come to believe they exist.

It's only a game. Or is it? Many people are watching and cheering as if it were a common sporting event. Others, like me, are both entertained and horrified. Must a show meant as satire result in so many injuries? I always come to the same conclusion: Lancaster's most thought-provoking activity is on roller skates.

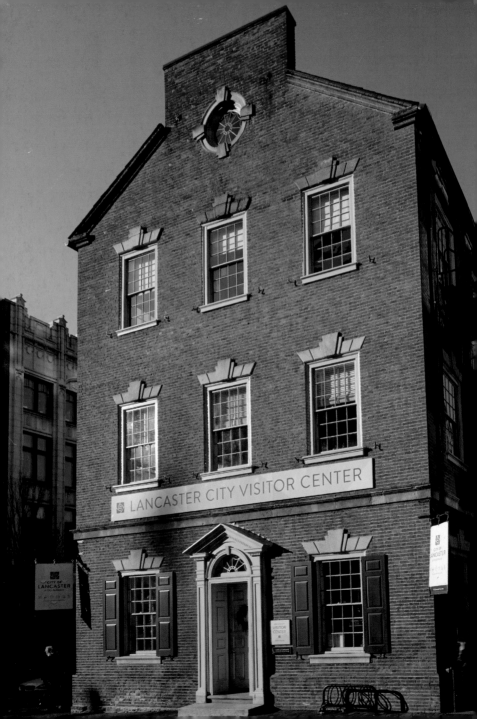

APPENDIX

Finding Local Information

LANCASTER CITY VISITOR CENTER

8 Penn Square, Lancaster

www.visitlancastercity.com

The visitor center is in Lancaster's oldest commercial building, which served as its first city hall during the colonial period. Across the alley from Central Market (page 79) and facing Penn Square, the red-brick building has been perfectly restored.

If you're beginning your journey downtown, this is a good place to get your bearings. The staff members know both the city and the countryside. They can help you find theater tickets, walking tours, and restaurants. And they make Sunday activity suggestions enthusiastically.

While they won't book a hotel room for you or be able to offer the sort of theological depth that the Mennonite Information Center can (next page), they're a great stop if you're downtown and have a question. Plus, you'll enjoy those video screens framed to look like paintings, featuring actors portraying local notables James Buchanan, General John F. Reynolds, Charles Demuth, and, in a double portrait, Lydia Hamilton Smith and Thaddeus Stevens. It's utterly charming; however, I felt pity for the models assigned to portray Thaddeus and Lydia. Tommy Lee Jones and S. Epatha Merkerson did such a vivid job in *Lincoln* that nobody could come close.

LANCASTER MENNONITE INFORMATION CENTER

2209 MILLSTREAM ROAD, LANCASTER

WWW.MENNOINFOCENTER.ORG

The Mennonite Information Center isn't only for the casual visitor. The exhibits showing Mennonite life and history require a bit of reading and concentration. For example, they have an English-language edition of the *Martyr's Mirror*, the Mennonites' most important historical book, out and open to a random page. Like every other random page I checked out, it told stories of gruesome death. Beheaded with the sword . . . eighteen tortured and sentenced to the fire. Next to the book is a sign inviting you to "relax in the reading room."

On the other hand, you can ask any question about the Mennonite faith and get an informed answer. No need to pay admission, make an appointment, or explain why you're asking. And if you don't have a question, this is still a great place to begin a deep dive into the culture.

Exhibits tell the story of the Mennonite faith and clearly explain their beliefs, including the differences between Mennonite and Amish theologies. This can be as dry as a truck repair manual in the wrong hands, but it's easily understandable here.

Downstairs are videos that share the Mennonite world view. In addition to watching a simple introductory film, you can pay to see a film called *The Lancaster Amish*. It could also be called "Disasters and the Lancaster Amish." A quarter of it is spent on the Nickel Mines school shooting, and much of the rest is on how the Amish deal with difficulties. It skips over what most outsiders want to hear about: the daily lives of Amish and Old Order Mennonites.

The wide selection of books ranges in topic from theology and ethics to local memoirs. If you're not ready for a thesis on Anabaptist thought, move on to the three rows of Amish romances. It's a bit jarring to see books by romance writer Beverly Lewis on shelves with theology texts, yet there they are. Women in white bonnets shoot concerned or caring looks from the covers. The authors know we're looking down on them, yet they're laughing all the way to the bank. No category sells more books than this one. And although these books aren't known for their authenticity regarding Amish life, the word is that Plain women devour them.

There's more to buy: toys and puzzles, plus gifts from a tiny outpost of the fair-trade chain Ten Thousand Villages. It will keep the shoppers in your group busy while you get your theological questions answered.

I am a regular churchgoer, but I was not prepared for the Tabernacle reproduction in a room behind the bookstore. For those of you who need a quick refresher, the Bible tells us that the Tabernacle was a tent, shrine, and dwelling place for God that the Children of Israel carried with them on their march through the desert. I paid a modest fee for the guided tour, and there it was, complete with a moving wax priest figure a tiny bit shorter and slimmer than I was.

I knew only a little about the Tabernacle, and if the model had included a taco truck and a video game arcade, I would have nodded silently in appreciation. However, my fellow tour goers seemed to know their Tabernacle history. Our guide, an earnest woman with an even-deeper knowledge of scripture, gave what seemed like a pretty good sermon on Exodus. Speaking without notes and in a tone one might use to describe the basics of particle physics to fifth-graders, her lecture came at us with charming clarity and supersonic velocity, though I got lost on the subplots.

As I studied the wax priest figure moving back and forth on its metal track, the discussion turned to the story of God giving the Children of Israel a gift of olive oil. This was a subject I knew something about, having done quite a bit of research on olive oil and its provenance! Furthermore, the sermons I'd heard at progressive houses of worship taught me that the Israelites had found a terrific place to grow olive trees, and they were thankful for this gift from God.

My comrades, however, seemed to believe that the gift of olive oil was instantaneous, as though a giant hand had appeared from the sky with a vat of oil symbolizing God's presence. Therefore, my questions about agriculture in the biblical era seemed to indicate disbelief on my part. I wanted to have a greater understanding of how things were grown at the Tabernacle, and my intentions were deeply misread. I was gripped with the feeling that a chasm was opening between me and the others. Our beliefs were each based on a lifetime of experience, and while our passions were equal, we stood on opposite sides of that canyon of faith.

For a moment, I felt superior, but that wax priest figure shot me a quick, cutting glance. Maybe in a more secular place, I could feel confident. But in Lancaster County, everybody's beliefs count, not just the ones you agree with. Plain people don't exist for our entertainment. Here, if you want to be respected, you have to do some respecting yourself.

Further Reading on the Amish

A huge number of books have been written about the Plain people of Lancaster County. They range from scholarly works to romance novels and can be found in local shops. While I have not explored the vast world of Amish romance, what I have read is *The Thrill of the Chaste: The Allure of Amish Romance Novels* by Valerie Weaver-Zercher (Johns Hopkins University Press, 2013). It's an intelligent exploration of the topic and will give sound answers to the many questions people have about this popular genre.

The late Stephen Scott's small and precise books offer what seems like an engineering manual for those trying to decipher the visible symbols of the Plain world. The diagrams of different bonnet styles in his *Why Do They Dress That Way* (Good Books, 2008) and his exacting descriptions of different buggy types in *Plain Buggies* (Good Books, 1998) make you realize the importance of each tiny detail.

Donald Kraybill is one of the top experts on Plain life and Anabaptist faith. While all of his books are worthwhile, *Simply Amish* (Herald Press, 2018) stands out as a basic introduction to their faith and philosophy. Kraybill is also coauthor, along with Steven Nolt and David Weaver-Zercher (husband of Valerie), of *Amish Grace*, a study of the Nickel Mines school shooting. This book takes a deep dive into the Amish perception of tragedy. Nolt has also written *A History of the Amish* (Good Books, 2016). While there are many more titles on the subject, this book is an ideal starting point.

If you choose the fiction route, be prepared for more books in more subcategories than you could imagine. The Amish are a sort of clean slate for authors; everybody knows a few basic rules, and a good novelist can flesh out the rest without anyone complaining. New genres of Amish fiction appear constantly. Just when you think the romance market is saturated, you'll hear about mysteries, science fiction, and vampires (*Amish Vampires in Space* by Kerry Nietz, Marcher Lord Press, 2013). Finally someone may tell you in a hushed voice about a volume they accidentally bought that turned out to be X-rated. When this happens, the only surprise is that you're not surprised.

Lancaster County Top-Ten List

My ten favorite Lancaster County places/activities, in no particular order.

1. Amish Meals at Home. The closest most of us will get to an Amish dinner table without converting and marrying into the family (page 23).

2. Wolf Sanctuary of Pennsylvania. A unique animal rescue facility in the wildest part of the county (page 102).

3. Country Housewares. Everything you need for the Plain life. If they don't sell it, Plain people probably don't use it (page 140).

4. Roller Derby. Plenty of up-close sports action and suitable for everybody. It's indoors too (page 175).

5. Old Windmill Farm. A rare chance to stroll the grounds of an Amish farm with the family that owns and runs it (page 50).

6. Lancaster Central Market. Both a food market and a farmers market, it provides a better sense of the land's bounty than anyplace else (page 79).

7. Groundhog Day at the Slumbering Groundhog Lodge. The festivities offer a strangely hilarious way to spend a bitterly cold February morning (page 66).

8. Covered bridges. Back roads are worth their own trip, even if you're not headed anyplace else (page 68).

9. Leola Produce Auction. Real farmers, real buyers, nothing trucked in from out of state (page 151).

10. Mud sales. Where Plain communities come out to play and invite everyone else to join them (page 154).

What to Do on Sundays

Nothing frightens a Lancaster resident more than the obligation to show a visitor around on a Sunday. So many things that give our county its charm are closed. You'll find the people who keep them open the rest of the week worshiping, socializing, and doing all the things people do when they're not running their business.

If you're interested in worship, you'll see that many churches have "Visitors Welcome" signs. I recommend that you stick with these. For our Plain residents, Sundays are a time to escape from the outside world, and your visit will be intrusive.

Beyond morning services, there's plenty to do on Sundays in Lancaster. Here are some suggestions:

• Amish Farm and House. There won't be any Amish people in residence on a Sunday, but staff members are on duty and there is plenty to see. (page 61)

• Buggy rides. On Sundays, buggy rides are offered without superfluous farm tours and cookie stops (page 58).

• Lancaster Polo Club. During the season, you can view a sporting event that's rarely so accessible in other places. It's a great picnic spot too (page 171).

• Miller's Smorgasbord. It's fancier than the others, and where else can you get glass of wine with your smorgasbord (page 22)?

• National Watch & Clock Museum. A unique collection and a fine way to spend a Sunday afternoon (page 107).

• State museums. Both the Ephrata Cloister (page 119) and Landis Valley Village and Farm Museum (page 129) have indoor and outdoor exhibits.

- Strasburg Rail Road. Check the online schedule. Their legendary shop tour is frequently offered on Sundays (page 116). The Railroad Museum of Pennsylvania across the street has Sunday hours too (page 111).

- Stoudtburg and the Antiques Mall. The huge antiques mall offers an eclectic shopping experience, and the private homes in the adjacent village are designed to evoke a European town (page 135).

- Wolf Sanctuary of Pennsylvania. Tours are often given on Sundays; check the website to make sure (page 102).

- Zoetropolis Cinema. If all else fails, take in a serious film (page 164).

- Any of the walks, parks, or trails can be a great place to spend a Sunday.

INDEX

Born in New York City and raised in the New York area, Brian Yarvin has been a commercial photographer for more than forty years. For the last fifteen years he's been combining photography and writing. Yarvin has contributed to publications such as the *Washington Post*, *Mothering*, SeriousEats.com, and *New Jersey Monthly*, to name a few. He has authored seven books on subjects ranging from Italian regional cuisine to New Jersey farmers to the history of lamb as a food. After long stints in Queens, New York, and Edison, New Jersey, he now lives in Lancaster, Pennsylvania.